LUTHER
vs.
POPE LEO

PAUL R. HINLICKY

LUTHER
VS.
POPE LEO

A CONVERSATION IN PURGATORY

Abingdon Press™

Nashville

LUTHER VS. POPE LEO:
A CONVERSATION IN PURGATORY

Copyright © 2017 by Abingdon Press

This book is printed on acid-free paper.

Library of Congress Cataloging-in-Publication Data has been requested.

ISBN: 978-1-5018-0420-5

Unless otherwise indicated, all scripture quotations are from the Common English Bible. Copyright © 2011 by the Common English Bible. All rights reserved. Used by permission. www.CommonEnglishBible .com.

Scripture marked as NRSV is from the New Revised Standard Version of the Bible, copyright 1989, Division of Christian Education of the National Council of the Churches of Christ in the United States of America. Used by permission. All rights reserved.

Quotations from *Declaration on the Way: Church, Ministry, and Eucharist* courtesy of Augsburg Fortress, copyright 2015.

Quotations from the *Joint Declaration on Justification* by the Lutheran World Federation and the Catholic Church courtesy of Wm. B. Eerdmans, copyright 2000.

Unless otherwise noted, all references to *Luther's Works* are from Jaroslav Pelikan, Helmut T. Lehmann, and Christopher Boyd Brown, eds., 75 vols. (Philadelphia: Muhlenberg and Fortress, and St. Louis: Concordia, 1955–). Hereafter, all references to *Luther's Works* will be cited as *LW* with the corresponding volume and page number.

17 18 19 20 21 22 23 24 25 26—10 9 8 7 6 5 4 3 2 1
MANUFACTURED IN THE UNITED STATES OF AMERICA

To friend and conversation partner, Fritz Oehlschlaeger, with whom I shall undoubtedly spend much time in purgatory!

CONTENTS

PREFACE

There must be a place in contemporary theology for thought experiments, such as the author now lays before the reader. Experienced hands regularly report that in the cold of this present ecumenical winter the doctrinal dialogues that arose after Vatican II have run their course and accomplished what they can. Supposedly we are now awaiting the long, slow march of "reception" through our hide-bound institutions. So why not a little play to pass the time? Perhaps even speed the process? Granted, I am playing with fire that can burn! But are we so satisfied with where we are that a little creative destruction cannot possibly help? It was tongues of fire, we are told, that descended on disciples hiding behind closed doors and pushed them out on the wind into the open to dream dreams and see visions. There are certain orthodoxies in academic and in ecclesial theology that squeeze this little space for experimentation so small that the smoldering wick gets smothered. But the flame of the divine Spirit creates its own oxygen. To switch the metaphor, the holy dove needs rooms to stretch wings and take flight into worlds that have not been but could yet be.

Let me confess right up front: I am no stylist. Genre-wise, I have birthed some kind of a monster in what follows: neither history nor theology but some fanciful, or, if you will, creative hybrid of the two that I am tempted to call an "ecumenical fantasy"—if the invocation of *fantasy* would not confuse contemporary readers all the more. As fanciful as putting Luther and Leo X together in an interminable purgatory may seem, I, in any case, mean what I say in the following with all the claim on mind and also Christian conscience that I and the story I have spun can muster. So maybe the tale falls into the genre of apocalyptic story like Daniel or prophetic fiction like Jonah. I don't know! Let the reader decide!

I do know that the author is a Lutheran. I think that is well known. But he is not of the wagon-circling type, sworn to eternal opposition to the papal antichrist. I think that is well known as well. Admittedly in what follows this Lutheran author can and will be accused, by certain Catholic readers of wagon-circling persuasion, of putting many things on the lips of Leo unjustified by strict historical science. If it will be of any comfort, let them assuredly know that certain Lutheran readers of the same wagon-circling proclivity will accuse the author of precisely the same crime regarding the Luther who appears in what follows. How else could he tell the story of their sojourns together in purgatory? It is not a revelation that the author claims for his tale. It is his invention, inspired perhaps but in any case well grounded in history and theology. As we shall see in conclusion, he lets the reader—indeed he forces the reader—decide about these questions as well.

The genesis of the book is simply explained. Abingdon Press editors asked if I would contribute to a series of this motif, expositing classical standoffs in theology[1]; they asked for a book on Luther versus the Pope for the anniversary year 2017. As I am not eager to reinflame this antiquated but still, as acknowledged above, inflammatory polemic, I hemmed and hawed. I had learned long ago from Jaroslav Pelikan that while "Rome has never really listened to the witness of the Reformation,"[2] that very deafness was potentially to be overcome in our time with the Second Vatican Council and its decree on ecumenism, *Unitatis Redintegratio*.[3] At the same time, I saw that the unhealthy state of Protestantism today is due in part to its four hundred plus years of unthinking reaction against the very notions of catholicity and visible unity. Lacking more and more "catholic substance," as Paul Tillich once put it,[4] the "protestant principle" of individual conscience has consequently disintegrated the church into hundreds of competing sects, deeply polarized today into modernist and fundamentalist wings on the question of Christianity's relation to the modern world. Pelikan's pioneering book taught many Protestants to think positively for the first time of authentic Christian values uniquely preserved in Roman Catholicism, values that Protestants needed to recover. He taught Lutherans especially to think of the "*tragic* necessity of the Reformation":

> Partisans on both sides have difficulty acknowledging that the Reformation was indeed a tragic necessity. Roman Catholics agree that it was tragic, because it separated many millions from the true church; but they cannot see that it was really necessary. Protestants agree that it was necessary, because the Roman church was so corrupt; but they cannot see that it was such a great tragedy after all.[5]

As I mulled the matter over, a brainstorm befell me, not unlike the lightning bolt that struck at law student Luther and chased him into the monastery. I had been working on the Ninety-Five Theses and was struck by how Catholic the argument actually is—more Catholic than the pope, so to say (well, in the Renaissance Florentine case of Giovanni de Medici, who became Leo X, that is not such a stretch). Professor Timothy Wengert, in a little book recently published on the Ninety-Five Theses, reported how a contemporary Lutheran layman pronounced, upon reading the famous text that ignited the great controversy of five hundred years ago, "It's not very Lutheran!"[6] A curious but revealing comment! Perhaps it is contemporary Lutherans who are not, well, "very Lutheran."

In any event, the insight that broke through was how Luther, in the theses, put the indulgence merchants on the horns of a dilemma: If purgatory is punitive, meant to satisfy divine justice before admission to heaven, and if the pope really has the power to relax such punishment, why not out of Christian love, as Scripture says, set the prisoners free—for free? An act of great generosity, alas, but not so lucrative, Luther insinuated. If, however, purgatory is purification, the Spirit preparing the redeemed to enter the presence of the holy God, what true Christian would ever short-circuit the process with a bribe, howsoever painful the purification needed to be?[7] Taking the latter horn up as the early Luther's affirmative "theology of the cross,"[8] I thought, why not take this "catholic" Luther up on the offer and put him together with Leo in the Spirit's purgatory, that is to say, confined together to quarters *as* their purgatory?[9] And so this book was born to tell in a popular form the progress that has been made since

Vatican II, which allowed Pope Francis to issue the following statement in his recent authorization of the liturgy for the Week of Prayer for Christian Unity in 2017: "Separating that which is polemical from the theological insights of the Reformation, Catholics are now able to hear Luther's challenge for the church of today, recognizing him as a 'witness to the gospel.' And so after centuries of mutual condemnations and vilification, in 2017 Lutheran and Catholic Christians will for the first time commemorate together the beginning of the Reformation."[10] May such time together in prayer and dialogue examine memories and purify desire!

Needless to say, straining out the polemic on both sides is a tall order. My tale cannot cover everything, especially not the developments since the time of Luther and Leo that have exacerbated the schism of the Western church. The tale told depends on bracketing such important problems to get back to the root of the divergence. Even so, the deep and careful historical and theological scholarship that has gone into the ecumenical and bilateral Lutheran-Catholic dialogues in the years since Vatican II fills a small library (*really*—I am thinking of the library at the Institute for Ecumenical Research in Strasbourg). And its fruit is represented on the lips of Luther and Leo in what follows by the device of italicizing direct quotations from the convergence documents approved by the churches; here, as elsewhere, the endnotes may be consulted for further study. In any case, a definite reduction in scope and simplification of issues is dramatized—even exaggerated in what follows—to make the point that at this hopefully *late* stage of ecumenical winter, *Lent* in the church year, our penance *together* in the Spirit prepares us for life from the dead and entry into a world that does not yet exist.

There are occasions in what follows when the omniscient narrator drops his veil and breaks into contemporary commentary. I hope these transitions are not overly jarring. The veil is dropped completely in the book's brief conclusion.

I am grateful to several friends who have read the manuscript and given me detailed commentary, saving me from mistakes and pushing the clumsy academic prose toward greater clarity in meaning as also felicity in style. Fritz Oehlschlaeger in particular provided detailed comments from the multiple perspectives he enjoys as a retired professor of English literature, a Christian ethicist, and an erstwhile Lutheran who has worshipped at Catholic mass for the last fifteen years—just the kind of guy I would like to spend purgatory with! This book is dedicated to him. In the meantime, we meet on earth to drink our local craft beer, antechamber of heaven in its own way and foretaste of the Banquet that awaits us all.

Paul R. Hinlicky
Epiphany 2017

NOT AS EXPECTED

History did not turn out as Luther had expected. His "prince"—that is to say, one of the chief hereditary rulers in German-speaking regions who also belonged to the "electors" of the Holy Roman Empire—had procured for him safe passage to the imperial assembly (called a "diet") in the city of Worms. There his case would be heard before a civil court of his own people, the Germans. He would not be forced to appear in Rome, as the papal indictment charging him with heresy required, to face trial there before a hostile audience.

In Luther's mind, an audience in Rome could not help but be hostile. Chief among his alleged heresies was a challenge in principle to the sole authority of the bishop of Rome as pope to judge him. In the beginning, however, challenging the unquestionable authority of the bishop of Rome to judge had not been Luther's motive in critiquing the sale of indulgences. The sale of indulgences promising, as its salesmen claimed, deliverance from the flames of purgatory in exchange for a financial gift indeed claimed the name and authority of the pope. His emblem, with the graphic of the keys to the kingdom granted to Peter and his successors, accompanied the salesmen (witness the ubiquitous joke about Peter, gatekeeper with the keys, greeting the deceased at the Pearly Gates). But in the beginning, Luther argued to the contrary that the sale of indulgences subverted the true and pastoral authority of the Roman pontiff. His early opponents—not in Rome, but in Germany—had quickly switched the

1

subject and made papal authority the central issue as they lost ground in the argument over indulgences. That being the case, Rome could not be an impartial judge, for Rome, or more precisely, the papal institution in Rome, had become party to the dispute. So Luther reasoned in any event.

Luther did not, however, think himself beyond error, as he expressly and repeatedly had asked to be shown his errors on the basis of Scripture and evident reason. To the extent that this posture of intellectual humility was sincere, he could at least wager on a more sympathetic hearing before peers at home, where for a variety of reasons resentment at the imperious ways and pecuniary appetite of the Roman papacy was widespread, if also inchoate. So Luther had traveled to Worms with a reasonable hope that whatever the diet decided about his Christian orthodoxy, he would be allowed time to reconsider all the questions involved while returning home safely to Wittenberg to await the outcome of events.

But it did not happen this way. His prince, Elector Frederick, who had arranged the safe passage for Luther, was enticed behind the scenes by overtures from the pope[1]; he secretly agreed to betray Luther for immediate execution following a pro forma hearing before the imperial diet.

Frederick betrayed Luther in exchange for the prospect, at the pope's suggestion of his support, of being elected the new emperor. At this time, the Luther affair was not the first thing on the minds of the assembled electors and their entourages, but rather the succession to the imperial throne. Indeed, these chief princes were called "electors" because the position of emperor was not hereditary, even though the sitting Emperor Maximillian wanted his Habsburg grandson, Charles, who had recently been sent to Spain from the Netherlands, to succeed him. Maximillian was aged. The chief item on the minds of the assembled at Worms was the politics of succession.

Neither was the Luther affair the chief preoccupation of the pope.[2] He had an enormous stake in the outcome of the diet as he struggled to procure the political independence of the papacy within Europe and therewith the unity of warring Christendom—reciprocating goals in his mind. His solution was to advocate a new Christian crusade against the encroachment from the east of the Muslim Turks, whose armies had entered Hungary and menaced Vienna.[3] The pope's vision, the lineage of which can be traced back in history to the victory of Charles "The Hammer" Martel over the Arab Muslim attempt to advance from Spain into France eight centuries before,[4] was one of Christian Europe united under the spiritual leadership of the pope against infidel Islam.[5]

In this connection, not least of Martin Luther's offenses in the pope's eyes was a politically provocative statement from his explanations of the Ninety-Five Theses, which had ignited the affair several years before. Whoever resists the Turk resists God, for the Turk, Luther had written, is God's rod to punish us wicked Christians for our sins.[6] If followed, such heretical counsel, so the pope thought, would portend the end of Christendom and the Islamization of Europe.

What was needed to save Christendom was to strengthen the papacy by preserving it from political interference[7] in a free and independent Italy, so that it could be in a position to lead Christian nations to peace within and together to victory over external enemies. The danger to Christendom was "secularization," in the sense that the leading institution of the church could be captured by secular powers and so made a pawn in the hands of the competing political factions of this world.[8] Giovanni de Medici, the first of the Medici popes from illustrious Florence, had inherited a papacy still wounded from the Great Schism of more than a century before, when rival popes were in sad fact pawns in the hands of the competing national-political powers.[9] Like his immediate predecessor, "The Warrior" Pope Julian II, Leo invested his energies in a flurry of diplomatic and military efforts to secure the papacy's independence within Europe by surrounding Rome with a cordon of "papal states" stretching from Milan in the north of Italy to Naples in the south. Yet others among the emerging nation-states of Europe of his time also coveted these Italian possessions, chiefly, as the pope feared, Charles of Spain who could become even more powerful as emperor of the German lands.

The German lands were loosely united in the Holy Roman Empire. Here, going back to Charlemagne, the grandson of Charles Martel, pope crowned emperor as heir to a "new,"—that is, "holy"—Roman empire.[10] It was the original alliance of "throne and altar," though in reality this model had deep precedent in the Christianization of Europe during the so-called Dark Ages. The tribes of Europe were Christianized in a complex symbiosis of nation-building and political centralization. Political sovereignty arose in tandem with Christian sacralization. The result was emergent *Christendom*. Peter Brown gives a crisp account of the Christian theological problem involved in muted but unmistakable terms:

> A small body of clergymen (notably Alcuin…) were challenged by [Charlemagne's] brusqueness to restate, more forcibly than even before, a view of Christian missions which emphasized preaching and persuasion. But, in fact, when it came to Charlemagne's treatment of the Saxons, most later writers took no notice of Alcuin's reservations. They accepted the fact that, as befitted a strong king, Charlemagne was entitled to preach to the Saxons "with a tongue of iron"—as a later Saxon writer put it without a hint of blame. Force was what was needed on a dangerous frontier. Education began, rather, at home. In the reigns of Charlemagne and his successors, a substantially new Church was allied with a new political system, both of which were committed, to a quite unprecedented degree, to the "correction" and education of their subjects.[11]

After eight centuries, however, the Christendom model had become wobbly. Other powerful political actors were now appearing on the European scene: the expulsion of the Muslims from Spain and the discovery of the new world had catapulted Spain to a leading position alongside traditional powerhouse France. Henry VIII reigned over the emerging naval power of England. All these chief actors, and a host of minor ones, vied for gain and glory in a confusing welter of claims with intersecting temporal and spiritual pretensions.

It was in this contestation, unbeknown to Luther, that Leo X, desperate to fend off the election of Charles of Spain whom he thought to have ambitions for Naples, had won Frederick to his cause. The pope secretly intimated support for Frederick's election to the imperial throne (while double-dealing the same intimations to King Francis of France[12]) on the condition that he quash the Luther movement, which had ignited on and was spreading from his territory of Saxon Germany.

As a result, like Jan Hus before him at the Council of Constance, Luther was betrayed at the diet of Worms and burned at the stake for his heresies. The unity of Christendom was thus preserved and the Muslim advance halted, when as an immediate result imperial winner Frederick and loser Francis of France united to defeat the Turkish armies in Hungary. Yet the secularization of the papal church into a pawn of imperial and/or national-political interests in the process was not checked. By the very mechanism of these machinations, the papacy had been reduced in fact to little more than a minor actor among the rising nation-states of Europe, its claim to spiritual leadership falsified by Leo's transparently political calculations.[13] History did not turn out as expected also for Leo X.

For upon his election to succeed Maximillian, the "wise" (as he was called) Frederick not only quashed the Lutheran movement but also turned his wrath on the papal party throughout the Holy Roman Empire. In politics, turnabout is fair play, and having witnessed the pope's calculation and double-dealing, Frederick felt few compunctions. The one element of Luther's message that had convinced him was the nationalist argument about Germany being fleeced by Rome by exploiting the superstitions of the population. Chief among the fleeced, Frederick came to realize, was he himself who had spent treasure upon treasures collecting alleged relics of Mary and the saints. Delivered from this "superstition," it was only just, he now reasoned, to return church properties to the ownership of the secular state from which they had been stolen by playing on the superstitious fears of the people. In this way, Luther's "unintended reformation" survived his own betrayal.[14]

Frederick reconciled Francis by giving him a leading position in the crusade against Islam, and he in turn emulated Frederick's policy of subordinating religion to interests of state. Frederick aligned the empire with Henry VIII of England against Spain several years later, since Spain remained nominally subordinate to the papacy, even though Charles, unbeknown to him, had been cheated out of the throne of emperor. In the process, the church *in* England and *in* Germany became respectively the churches *of* England and *of* Germany, "people's churches."[15] The papacy fared no better in attempts to ally with Spain. Charles in Spain consoled his loss of the empire by freeing himself utterly of Catholic moral restraints in a policy of total colonization of the newly discovered world across the Atlantic Ocean.

Yet Leo X did not live to see any of this. He, too, died before the consequences of unintended "counter-reformation" became visible. Enjoying his favorite pastime in the marshy lowlands outside of Rome hunting wild boar, Leo received word by messenger of Luther's execution. So elated was the weak-eyed Leo at the news that he dismounted and took up the spear to finish off a cornered boar. But his stroke missed the target, and the portly pope fell forward into the tusk of the boar. It was not a pretty sight.

Eternity did not turn out as either Luther or Leo had expected.

Mercifully the smoke had asphyxiated Luther before the terrible pains of death by burning could deliver further cruelties upon his body, already seething with pain as the torturers had sought to procure from the condemned man a last-minute retraction of his heresies. But Luther had not recanted, firm in his belief that he would pass instantaneously into the company of the white-robed martyrs above. But as Luther awoke from death's sleep, he seemed alone on his bed in a plain, gray, windowless room. He wondered at his whereabouts.

Purgatory, too, was not quite as he imagined it. Truth be told, he had come in the course of the controversy to doubt that a postmortem purgatory even existed; already from the beginning he was demythologizing purgatory and giving it an existential interpretation. "Since we believe that peace, joy and confidence reign in heaven in the light of God," he had explained, "we also believe that in hell despair, grief and terrible flight rage." Between these two, purgatory, Luther continued, "is nearer hell than heaven, for in purgatory there is a despair, a longing to escape, dread, and grief." He quickly qualified, however, "*near* despair, for that type of despair finally comes to an end... [though] it does not feel capable of hope. The Spirit alone helps them in their weakness."[16] In tandem with such existential interpretation of purgatory as the Spirit's work in a refining furnace, Luther had long doubted those lurid pictures of its cruel torments that his opponent, the Dominican friar John Tetzel, merchant of papal indulgences, had conjured up to frighten gullible people into rescuing their loved ones by means of a financial donation.

In principle Luther argued against a purely penal purgatory supposedly satisfying divine justice with pain in compensation for crime for the sake of a true and spiritual purgation of the Christian penitent. Luther's Ninety-Five Theses, which had gotten him into all this trouble, seemed already at the time to be making an argument against a purely post-mortem purgatory in favor of a present, real-time purification of desire. The message announced in its first thesis, "When our Lord and Master Jesus Christ said, 'Do penance,' he meant for the entire life of the believer to be one of repentance," was intended as, and taken to mean, something like, "Purgatory *without delay*! Purgatory *now*!"

So Luther awoke, proven half-right right that purgatory was not a cruel place of penal satisfaction for crimes. But only half-right. He had sought to put Tetzel's preaching of purgatory on the horns of a dilemma. As salvation is not deliverance from sin's *punishment*, but deliverance from *sinful desire*, any true Christian delivered from sin by the conversion of the heart's desire *welcomes* sin's "punishment" as spiritual exercises in the *mortification* of the old Adam, as the divine Holy Spirit's own "crucifixion" of the flesh. Luther's gospel had not been that God spares from punishment, but that the God who spared not His own Son leads those united with His Son through death with Him into newness of life. The *good* news is that the sinner *gets* to die with Christ and so arise in Christ to a life of battle, into a world in which sin is still present and afflicting but now no longer reigns free and unfettered in the baptized. Thus the entire life of the Christian on earth is an earnest battle, a living and present purgatory!

If purgatory is real, then, true Christians welcome it rather than flee from it in terror, as the very fulfillment of their new, Spirit-given desire for purification. For unless evil desire is healed, it is impossible to enter heaven.[17] But if, instead, purgatory satisfies divine justice by inflicting punishment on sins as the indulgence preachers maintain, and if the pope has at his disposal a vast treasury of surplus merit from Jesus, holy Mother Mary, and all the saints that he can credit to the deficit accounts of needy sinners suffering dire punishment to satisfy justice, Luther asked, why doesn't the pope in Christian love just give it all away? Set the prisoners free with free pardon? If he is able to do this but instead sells the credit, he is a spiritual usurer, making a profit from work not his own. What a blow to the reputation of the pope's pastoral office, Luther slyly noted, as smart laypeople are beginning to question!

More deeply, Luther had argued, the root idea of surplus merit at the disposition of the pope betrays the true treasure of the church: "For Christ is the Ransom and Redeemer of the world, and thereby most truly and solely the only treasury of the church."[18] It is true that good works are necessary for salvation even though they are not in the power of weak humans captivated by sinful desire. But the one good work that suffices for all was the obedience of Jesus Christ to death, even death on a cross, for those disabled by their captivation to self-seeking in all things. That is why He[19] is called the "ransom." By this His work of love seeking others and not Himself, He has gained the salvation of all who abandon their own self-seeking efforts at self-salvation and instead surrender to His searching love. This treasure is the good news of the generosity of God in giving salvation in Christ, so costly to God, yet freely given to those not deserving. It is the gift, then, which in its human reception does what it says in transforming human desire just as the Apostle Paul had once written that he now wanted to "be found in him. In Christ I have a righteousness that is not my own and that does not come from the Law but rather from the faithfulness of Christ. It is the righteousness of God that is based on faith" (Phil 3:9).

Awakening then to the place of his final purification, Luther was not wrong about the need for truth and reconciliation through a process of purgation of sinful desire. But he was wrong to think that it had no future dimension, particularly in his own case. As judgment begins in the household of God, purgatory awaits each believer for refinement, as dross is separated from gold in the furnace. Luther awoke in further need of completing his repentance, though in his postmortem drowsiness he could not yet grasp this.

As he rose from his bed in the dim room, another bed appeared to him from the opposite corner. Rolling over on his side to greet Luther was Giovanni de Medici, also known as Pope Leo X. Although they had never met face-to-face in life, they immediately knew each other. The shock in each struck to the core of their beings. Neither could fathom what recognition of the other could signify in these strange new whereabouts. Each had expected the other to be damned, just as each expected vindication for himself. But here they had awoken in each other's presence, confined to quarters together, as it appeared.

Leo had gone hunting to escape—as he often needed to do—the debilitating tensions of his papal office. All his shrewd diplomacy was backfiring, he feared. He knew from the long history of Christianity in Europe that the warring tribes of the Dark Ages had been civilized by the labors of the missionary monks. He knew that the long, slow march to civilization had been ministered by the church. The project of a new and "holy" Roman Empire arising from the ruins of the ancient pagan order was the progressive work of God and his own culminating vision of Christianity in history. As the barbarian warlords incorporated the monasteries and convents within their fortress walls, these newly emerging forms of political sovereignty purchased divine sanction and superior religious power to that possessed by the old paganisms. The educational ministry of the church prepared future political leaders with literacy and a sense of historical purpose. In turn, the church gained privileged access to the common people.

"Whoever the ruler, his the religion" became a motto for cultural truce in the so-called Wars of Religion that emerged a century after the time of Luther and Leo, but it was already common coin going back to imperial Rome, where from the time of Julius Caesar the emperor was also *pontifex maximus*, or "chief priest."[20] Julius embodied the transition of Rome from republic to military dictatorship. Having perfected the art of crucifixion as a tool of colonial subjugation, he returned from Gaul to Rome to buy the title of chief priest through a bold strategy of bribery, knowing that the control of religion was tantamount to the control of culture. Christianity in the West since the time of Augustine centuries later, however, had complicated this Julian imperial synthesis with the idea of the two "societies": the earthly city and the city of God living together in tension until the separation of the sheep and goats at the Last Judgment. Through the medieval period of Christendom this tension between the two cities imperfectly manifested itself in the tug of war between pope and emperor. Despite Luther's reformatory attempt to draw the line between the two cities through church and state alike rather than between them, the aforementioned "unintended" secularization of Christendom followed. The imperial incorporation of religion begun with Julius Caesar, interrupted by Augustine, slowly but steadily gained ground again after the time of Leo and Luther.

The deep problem was that baptizing the masses did not immediately convert and pacify them. United officially in a common or "catholic" Christianity, Europe remained beneath its baptismal veneer a hotbed of tribalism and internecine warfare. The tension between Augustine's two cities was thus manifested in the convoluted power conflicts between kings and emperors claiming divine right to political sovereignty and popes claiming temporal jurisdiction that they delegated to secular sovereigns, as Pope Leo III had crowned Charlemagne. While popes held up the banner of trans-ethnic Christian unity, in historical reality they often behaved—and had to behave—as one local political actor alongside others. Even prior to the Luther debacle, "warrior popes" such as Julius, Leo's immediate predecessor, had already thoroughly "secularized" the pastoral office for all with eyes to see. Yet in this to and fro of emperor and pope, it had been chiefly—if not only—the external threat of Islam that galvanized a Western Christian consciousness of Europe as a spiritual whole.

Leo was heir to this stew of contradictions. For him, the political meaning of the gospel was paramount and its sense evident from this now centuries-long project of building a new Christian civilization in Western Europe. The church was not a utopian "Platonic Republic" existing only in the mind or heart, but a real, on-the-earth, visible union in doctrine, rite, and morals sufficiently potent to ban inter-Christian warfare and to summon united Christendom to crusade against the infidel aggressors. Its temporal potency was the power claimed by the papacy to delegate political sovereignty; its spiritual power consisted in the administration of grace, necessary to escape hell and attain heaven, which spiritual power the pope could grant or retain according to his judgment for the sake of Christendom's civilizational mission. The "spiritual" threat of the "ban" (excommunication) by the administration of the "office of the keys" (emblazoned on the papal coat of arms) was potent magic indeed.

So in Leo's mind, the sale of indulgences was triply justified. First, it reinforced the claim that Christ had transferred the administration of grace to Peter and his successors, the bishops of Rome who were also popes of the universal church. Indulgences that administered divine pardon through the merit of Christ, Mary, and the saints were the popes' to give or retain, to sell or to gift as they saw fit. Second, indulgences for the Christian cause of crusade against the Muslim Turks incentivized recruitment and rallied public support, much like the sale of war bonds in modern times. Third, indulgences sold for the building of St. Peter's basilica in Rome visibly signified the spiritual unity of Europe in Christianity, for there in Rome the Apostles Peter and Paul had united in the martyr's deaths at the hand of the old and unholy Roman Empire, consecrating this place as the site of the Christian civilization's future capital.

But all his efforts to secure this grand narrative with its vision for the future were in fact collapsing in the final moments of Leo's life when he succumbed to the wild boar. To be sure, the Elector Frederick betrayed Luther to the flames at Leo's prompting. But the cynicism of the deal convinced Frederick of Luther's claim that Leo had no primary or even genuine care for spiritual things (as had the fanatically Christian monk Luther) but used religious ideas for political ambitions. So Frederick felt justified in doing the same.

Earlier in life Frederick was pious—so pious, in fact, that he had accumulated one of the largest collections of sacred relics in Europe. Luther's relentless preaching of salvation by the grace of God alone brought with it an equally relentless exposé of relic superstition. The scales fell from pious Frederick's eyes. What a waste of money, as now also in the sale of indulgences, at the hands of the sordid merchants of religion! To what better secular purposes could the vast riches be used, accumulated through the centuries in the landed estates and educational properties of religious institutions? Elected emperor, Frederick turned with equal and even more intense fury on the papal party in German lands, and he encouraged his peers in the rest of Europe to do the same. He welcomed the claim of his erstwhile rival, Charles of Spain, upon the papal state of Naples and cheered King Francis's repossession of Milan, shrinking the pope to a postage stamp state in the surrounds of Rome.

Yet in death Leo was still held by the religious conviction that he had inherited, and stewarded to the best of his ability, the great civilizational project of Christendom. As he awoke from death and rolled over on his side to discover his whereabouts, Leo was aghast, as Luther had been, in beholding his cellmate. On the table between them a document lay. Leo arose and took it up. After fumbling for his eyeglass, he read it and, shaking his head in disbelief, returned to his bed and rolled onto his side away from Luther. Luther then took up the document and began to read out loud, as was his custom when reading Latin.

"Christian brothers Leo and Martin! Welcome to the antechamber of heaven. Here you must prepare yourselves to enter the holy presence of God, spotless and blameless in His sight. This work in you now is the Spirit's merciful work for you, so that you may shine without stain in the radiance of God's glory when you are permitted to pass from this place. For as all have sinned and fallen short of the glory of God, each in his own particular way must be fashioned anew into the new creation.

"Leo, you have without justice pronounced your brother in Christ a heretic and condemned him to a painful and unjust death. Martin, you have without justice pronounced your brother in Christ an antichrist and damned him, as if you were the Last Judge over him. You are both in the wrong. You cannot pass into the presence of the holy God from this place of preparation until you reconcile these wrongs. This work of reconciliation is your purgatory. You cannot bribe your way out of this purgatory, not even by pleading the precious blood of Christ, let alone the merits of the saints. It is your own final salvation from sin that is at stake in this work. God grants you the Holy Spirit to bring His work in you to completion!

"As I, Peter, once quarreled with my brother in Christ, Paul, at Antioch, but reconciled with him at last in Nero's Coliseum, so you must now reconcile. I will be watching over you. If you have trouble in your assignment, the Spirit who ever hovers over you will send a helper. Adieu, until I greet you face-to-face."

Luther finished reading, crumpling the paper in his hands. He thought to himself: "I am now to dispute with the antichrist?" He burst out, "I'll be damned!"

The ashen-faced Leo turned to Luther and spit out the words, "That's for damn sure!"

Finally they had agreed on something. "Disputation"[21] was the scholastic method of thinking out controversies by a method of arguing pro and con propositions to test for the validity of the evidence considered and the logic of inferences drawn. Luther's Ninety-Five Theses were originally meant for such formal, academic "disputation," as they were composed in Latin for the audience of educated peers, not the masses, though popularization happened when Luther's text was pirated, translated into German, and circulated by earnest supporters and unscrupulous publishers. To be sure, like a modern-day tweeter bypassing self-appointed gatekeepers, Luther quickly learned from the success of the pirates and used the new printing press technology of his day to take his case directly to the masses. But the line between democracy and demagoguery then, as now, was thin to vanishing and ever shifting.

As educated men, Luther and Leo both knew the method developed in medieval universities to achieve rational agreement or, failing that, to clarify disagreement. In life, both Luther and Leo, however, had fallen short of a genuine meeting of the minds. They had, for differing reasons, fallen short of disputation and fallen instead into demagoguery and invective. For Luther, there was no disputing with antichrist; invective that weaponizes arguments to defeat an implacably malicious foe and rescue weak, ignorant, or wavering potential victims from the papal maw was the only course following his excommunication. Why, if Leo had condemned Luther's doctrine, he had condemned Augustine, no, Paul the apostle along with him, who else could antichrist be? Leo, too, would not dispute with a heretic. His pastoral duty was not rationally to convince a wild boar running amuck in the vineyard of the Lord, but to bring him to his knees by confronting him with the objective fact of his heretical teaching. If Luther should persist in mad heresy despite ample warning and assurance of mercy upon recantation, he would prove himself an incorrigible heretic.

Dispute with the antichrist? Never! Argue with the heresiarch? Impossible! They would rather be damned!

13

A BLESSED GRIEFWORK

A long silence followed, each alone in his thoughts. From the initial shock of their encounter, the prior fact itself of awakening to purgatory began to dawn on them. Leo had taken the precaution in life of acquiring for himself ample and extensive indulgences, which in theory should have brought him safely and without delay to Jordan's shore. Luther had come to the conclusion that a postmortem purgatory was nothing but a money-making invention of the papists and that he, as a martyr to this truth, would awaken at once in Abraham's bosom. The fact of their present placement testified to each that neither was wholly in the right—that somehow both were together in the wrong. Worst of all, the wrong had to do with each other!

They addressed each other gruffly when the silence was finally broken. "Heretic," Leo barked, "what are you doing here?"

"I am your eternal torment, antichrist!" growled Luther. Like a coiled snake, Luther had been waiting to strike when Leo finally broke the silence.

"Then you really are a devil here to torment me!" Leo snapped back.

"All right, then," Luther retorted, "I am God's devil to punish you for your sins." Luther almost spit the words at Leo.

Even in purgatory, Luther continued to think of himself as a prophet rather than an academic theologian who had been thrust by circumstances into a prophetic role. After all, his biblical research had taught him that

15

God spoke in riddles and parables, paradoxes and enigmas. How fitting, then, that as God's mouthpiece Luther, too, should speak in paradoxes! A delicious paradox, indeed, this new one, he mused: Luther put in purgatory, donning the mask of God's devil, to punish Leo for his sins! The self-justifying solution of the self-proclaimed prophet had come to Luther almost intuitively. Paradox makes perfect sense to the elect, but it baffles; indeed, it is meant to baffle the reprobate.

Another long silence ensued. Leo mused on Luther's self-aggrandizement, too clever by far: even in purgatory Luther was in the right, God's own whip eternally to lash him. Could no evidence ever convince Luther of error? Can paradoxical thinking swallow up every objection and turn it to advantage?

A paradox is a logical contradiction, like, say, "square triangle." It is impossible by definition of the terms involved. It collapses the law of non-contradiction, which in turn makes all reasoning futile. It yields nothing but nonsense and gibberish, no matter how passionately enunciated. "The Christian is righteous and sinner at the same time," Leo thought, recalling a notorious instance from the compendium of Luther's errors that seemed *both* to deny the infusion by the Spirit of grace in baptism, making the baptized righteous, *and* to concede victory in advance to sin. Or again the statement that the Christian is at the same time "lord of all and servant of everyone"—textbook instances of gibberish, to which one can say neither yes nor no because one cannot make out what is actually meant or claimed. Paradox—this was a strange way of thinking for Leo.

Finally, though, it occurred to him that two can play the paradox game. Turnabout is fair play. So Leo broke the silence: "By the same token, heretic, I am your devil, your torment, God's forever monkey on your back!" Luther was stunned at Leo's comeback. He had not considered *that* possibility; and for the first time in his life—well, in his postmortem existence—the prophet was rendered speechless.

As he grappled with Leo's turnabout, Martin realized that he had been put on the horns of a dilemma. If he stopped preaching paradoxes at the pope, he would have to dispute with him rationally in discursive fashion. If he disputed with him, he would have to regard him as a rational agent

16

and potential brother capable of persuasion. He might even have to settle, then, for an achieved disagreement rather than pure capitulation from the archenemy. If so, he would have to recognize that Leo was not the supernatural antichrist and that he had been in error in quite literally demonizing him so. Furthermore, he would have to exposit in the process his theological paradoxes to Leo with discursive reasoning. He would have to argue, not merely pronounce prophetic judgment, "Thus says the Lord..." like the prophets of old. True, Luther at that moment remained still in a state of cognitive dissonance from Leo's reversal and could not yet think out this series of steps. He only sensed that if he responded rationally and in good faith to Leo's turnabout, which had snared him in his own paradox, he would be opening up a long, weighty, and painful dialogue. That would indeed be his purgatory. Naturally, he was reluctant to do so. But finally the alternative prospect of eternal boredom in stoney mutual silence pushed him forward.

"So you are not the antichrist, for why would the antichrist be in purgatory at all? We in the Latin West know that the church in the East condemned the notion of universal salvation when it arose among the disciples of Origen, and how our Augustine especially confirmed that there is no hope of salvation for the devil and his servants. So that is clear. If you are in purgatory, you are among the number of the redeemed being prepared for the consummation. I cannot deny this evidence before my eyes. But if you are in purgatory in hope of final salvation, why are you together with me?"

Luther paused for his question to settle on Leo and then continued,

"I claim no merit of my own but cling solely to the merits of Christ for salvation. But you have condemned just this doctrine of the merit of Christ alone which He distributes gratis, hence by grace alone, as all-sufficing satisfaction for us and our salvation. You have upheld the sale and purchase of merits of Mary and the saints, not to mention the precious blood of Christ, for salvation on the double presumption that the saints would have surplus merit available and that their distribution would be at your disposal, not to mention the blasphemous presumption that you have the merits of Christ at your beck and call. This I cannot comprehend.

17

This much I say, then: you may not be the antichrist, as I had thought, but you are surely not the 'Holy Father' either, for your sins were many and chiefly those that I have just enumerated. But also alongside them is this sin, that you were no holy father to me."

These thoughts were an honest expression of Luther's convictions that had brought him to the pyre. He had held that the office of the papacy was to be the Western church's chief pastor,[1] "the highest and general priest of all priests,"[2] as this arrangement had evolved historically; like any other form of temporal government, this ecclesiastical system was worthy of human respect and obedience, subject to the higher allegiance owed to God alone. This is what Luther affirmed when he affirmed papal primacy *de jure humano*, but not *de jure divino* (lacking, as papal primacy seemed to him, a clear mandate of Christ). Indeed, at the beginning of the whole affair that had led to his condemnation, Luther perhaps naively but without doubt sincerely intended to defend Pope Leo along these lines against poisonous "flatterers"—the preachers of indulgences at home in Germany and in the papal court, "the curia." It was these latter, not Pope Leo, as Luther had repeatedly made clear in published writings, who were his opponents.

In his explanation of the Ninety-Five Theses, for example, Luther had written that "we now have a very good pope, Leo X, whose integrity and learning are a delight to all upright persons."[3] He expressed his confidence that the church's chief pastor, guided by the Holy Spirit, would recognize the teaching of the Apostle Paul and of the blessed Augustine in his writings against the merchants of indulgences and vindicate it. As a true pastor, he would rise up and judge against the "papist" flatterers, as Luther reminded Leo of the precedent of Bernard of Clairvaux's remonstration of Pope Eugenius III almost four centuries earlier, calling the pope to Christian humility.[4] He made the tacit distinction between the person and the office this way:

> It makes no difference to me what pleases or displeases the pope. He is a human being just like the rest of us. There have been many popes who have been pleased not only with errors and vices but even with horrible things. I listen to the pope as pope, that is, when he speaks in and according to the

canons, or when he makes a decision in accordance with a general council. I do not listen to him, however, when he speaks his own mind. In this way I am not compelled to say with certain people who hardly know the teachings of Christ that the horrible murders committed by Julius II among Christians might have been blessings by which he demonstrated to the flock of Christ that he was a true shepherd.[5]

A neat distinction, of which Catholics through the ages have not infrequently availed themselves. The "flatterers" close to home were the indulgence preachers in Germany, far from Rome, who used the pope's name and insignia to legitimate their traffic in the religion business. It was only at a later stage in the conflict, and then to deflect attention from Luther's claim that the true treasure of the Church is Christ's merit, costly won but freely given, that they changed to subject. They were rapidly losing ground in the public debate on the value and use of indulgences; so they upped the ante, arguing that in principle Luther's critique of indulgences entailed a rejection of papal authority. Indeed, they had wrangled out of Luther the admission that churches and councils as well as popes can err. And they took this case against Luther for subversion to Rome. Even so, almost to the very end, Luther held out hope that Leo would give him a hearing and decide in his favor. It was only when Leo had officially condemned his teachings as heresy that Luther drew the apocalyptic conclusion: if the pope condemns Luther's teaching, he condemns Paul and Augustine in Luther. Ergo, this must be the antichrist of prophecy, who takes his seat in the church of God (2 Thess 2:3-4).

A neat theory, but put to the test now in purgatory and so in need of some revision. It was dawning on Luther in this moment that clinging in trust to Christ's righteousness, not his own, was something to be distinguished from clinging to his theological ideas and verbal formulations about Christ's righteousness, costly gained but freely given. Right ideas, to be sure, are better than wrong ones. Yet they are always thought and formulated contextually from historically specific human perspectives and as such not capable of timeless universalization. Rather, they are available through a hermeneutical process of deconstruction and reformulation to speak again the same content and make the same witness in new locales under new circumstances.[6] What can be rightly required is not verbal identity of formulation but a rationally convincing demonstration of material continuity that intends "orthodoxy," that is, conceptualizations and formulations that successfully teach the same gospel of Jesus Christ, who is "the same yesterday, today, and forever!" (Heb 13:8).

Indeed, as Luther himself acknowledged,[7] no one is justified by having the right idea but rather by having in faith the reality to which the formulation refers or the idea conceptualizes; and ideas or concepts or doctrinal formulas can do their work to greater and lesser degrees of clarity and communicability in the act of referencing, which shows others what in the world one is talking about. One does not trust, therefore, in the idea but in the thing it signifies and expresses and comprehends. It is not faith in the doctrine of justification by faith that saves but faith in Jesus Christ our righteousness. And the idea does not work as a good idea, if it does not work to communicate this reference and explicate its meaning clearly and distinctly and effectively. That's a difficulty with Luther's favored form of theologizing—the paradox—which is a rhetorical form, a peculiar kind of metaphor that veritably demands conceptual interpretation.[8] Preaching paradox like "Christ crucified" (i.e., Victor victimized) can be arresting, but it is not convicting if one never comes to understand who it is on the road to Damascus who has knocked you off your high horse and why.

A paradox is a rhetorical figure of apparent contradiction that works to generate a new meaning in the world for which there is no suitable existing vocabulary. A jarring paradox can disrupt customary thinking and shake up accumulated ideas to show the way to new things needing new words. So one could say Christ is the Lamb, meaning not that Christ is wandering after his mother in a pasture somewhere but that Christ is the Priest who offers Himself, not another, for the sake of others. "Christ is the Lamb of God" can thus work a salutary cognitive dissonance that opens closed minds to new meaning. But it can also remain a riddle. As such it can exasperate and close minds, if it is not interpreted patiently, which is what Christian teaching is and does. A muddied sign cannot signify and a self-contradictory idea cannot explain.

Consequently, clinging to one's existing ideas is questionable, since there may be better ones that conceptualize the reality that concerns one more clearly and distinctly; this is especially the danger when the rhetorical figure insists upon itself as if it were a self-explanatory concept. In this case the supposed idea functions more to obscure than to clarify. If one's only response to the blank look upon the face of one's auditor is to persist in paradoxical pronouncement in an ever-louder and angrier voice, when patient disputation is required instead, one either stupidly or willfully frustrates communication. The impatience of the prophet combined with the self-righteousness of the orthodox—for Luther paradoxically thought of himself as the "heretic" who was truly orthodox—is a subtle serpent.

But Leo was not privy to these reflections going on in Luther's mind. Instead, a humbled Leo muttered softly, almost inaudibly, "Yes, I know my sins are many. You know I was raised from birth by my illustrious family to become pope someday. I was made a prince of the church at the age of seven![9] And I labored quietly and patiently under that warrior Julius II. His bloody crimes, I do concede in fear and trembling, were countless.[10] I, in fact, absolved immediately the French nobility for ecclesiastical disobedience, when King Francis told me, 'Your Holiness must not be surprised that all these men hated Julius II, for he was our greatest enemy; in all our wars we have no enemy as terrible as he, for Julius II was indeed a most capable general and far better suited to be such than to be pope.' Thus I remember in the documentation collected for your case that somewhere you described him as a 'murderer,' and I know all too well how you were right about that. But I was his understudy and kept quiet, biding my time patiently, believing in Providence.[11] And what of fate had been mine! Banished, imprisoned, liberated, at one time Lord of Florence, and now Supreme Head of the Church! What wonder that men of letters—even you, Luther, early on—could not tire of extolling this favorite and conqueror of fortune in verse and inscription.[12]

"My reputation as a morally virtuous person was not wholly underserved,"[13] Leo continued, "as you also once acknowledged. Indeed, if I remember rightly from the same documents, you too expressed admiration for me as a person of sanctity; my reputation at least at the beginning of my reign was universally acknowledged. Yes, it was so. Indeed, when I was elected after Julius's unlamented death, I wanted to change directions.[14] On my first Maundy Thursday as pope, I made a point of kissing the feet of the poor, saying that the ceremony ought to take place in reality and not only in appearance.[15] I wanted wars to cease among Christian nations. I found this fact of internecine Christian warfare mortifying. I sought a culturally and spiritually renewed papacy after the embarrassing schism of the fourteenth century, after political captivity, after papal warfare. I wanted my papacy able to lead Europe morally and effectively to negotiate conflicts among Christians.

"For me it became a matter of urgency that we Christians unite in crusade against the invading Turks. These Muslim infidels had swallowed up Byzantium and crept up the Balkans, occupied Catholic Hungary, and were now knocking on Vienna's door. There was a moment of weakness, given to us by God, as I supposed, when the Sultan Selim was entangled in Egypt in 1516. Now, I preached, we should carry out God's cause and uniting ourselves, attack the Turks under the unfurled banner of the Holy Cross![16] My earnestness in this was beyond question.[17] I was much preoccupied with this Islamic threat and the succession to the imperial throne when your affair came along. Truth be told, you were to me little more than a distraction raising up novel doctrines and fomenting a theological dispute among the ever-quarrelsome monks on matters long settled by the sanctified habits of sacred tradition.

"Yet now I see how all my efforts were futile. By preferring diplomacy to war, I became entangled in diplomatic intrigues and double-dealing; and when that failed, even I fell into a brutal and expensive war against the Duke of Urbino. I was so caught up in this campaign that I barely noticed the hypocrisy when Italian canons asked what good was the law forbidding priests to stain their hands with blood, since now—speaking *of me, not* Julius II—they complained, popes and cardinals have become antichrists and tyrants![18] The need for funds colored my judgment. The sale of indulgences was lucrative. When your elector, Prince Frederick, betrayed you to the flames, however, he would next betray me and return the papacy to political subjugation. I didn't succeed in uniting Christendom against Islam. I didn't succeed in renewing the papacy.

"As if all this were not woe enough, my own cardinals conspired to assassinate me![19] I should have realized that this event provided a deeper insight into the intense corruption of the highest ecclesiastical body.[20] But my solution was centralization.[21] While I forgave some of the conspirator cardinals, in a fit of rage I had the chief perpetrator, who was a mere child of twenty-two years, cruelly tortured before his execution.[22] And I then I purged the College of Cardinals and stacked it with rich sycophants who would solidify my power within the church, though alas not, as mentioned, among the nations. The thought that Francis and Charles might come to an understanding against me pursued me like a menacing spectre; the temporal power of the Holy See as a safeguard of its spiritual interests captured me, mind and heart.[23] Frustrated in every direction, I drifted away from the lavish living in Rome and the extravagance for which I was justly accused.[24] Toward the end I spent my time away from the city in hunting camp[25]; only there I was gouged to death by a wounded boar. *Sic transit gloria mundi. So passes the world's glory!*

"How did it end this way? I took my unlikely escape from French captivity in Julius's final war as an act of providence.[26] And when I was welcomed home to Florence after a long exile, I was elated at God's favor. And then in such quick succession to be elected successor to Julius. I can remember saying to my brother under this sunshine of divine favor, 'If God has seen fit to give us the papacy, let us by all means enjoy it!'[27] But my joy has now turned to sorrow. The Lord gave and the Lord has taken away!"

Unhappy at his fate, troubled in his conscience, Leo had just confessed sins to a heretic. The pathos did not escape the listening Luther, whose fierce heart even in life could quickly melt into an ocean of pastoral compassion.

"Brother Leo—if I may speak as man to man and Christian to Christian—one thing only I am now sure of. All our sins are Christ's—if only they displease us—and His righteousness in turn is ours. I explained this once in writing, but let me now say it you personally and directly:

23

a Christian can be glorified with Christ and can with confidence claim all things in Christ. Righteousness, strength, patience, humility, even all the merits of Christ are theirs through the unity of the Spirit by faith in him. All his sins are no longer his; but through that same unity with Christ everything is swallowed up in him. And this is the confidence that Christians have and our real joy of conscience, that by means of faith our sins become no longer ours but Christ's upon whom God placed the sins of us all. All the righteousness of Christ becomes ours. He places his hand upon us, and all is well with us. He spreads his cloak and covers us, blessed Savior throughout all ages.[28] When we come into the truth and confess, rather than protest our sins, then, something better than release from punishment is ours. This is what the Scriptures mean by the forgiveness of our *sins*, not simply or chiefly the pardon of deserved *punishment*, but the obliteration of the guilt that walls us off from those whom we have injured, beginning with God and extending to every creature. That forgiveness consists in embrace of the merciful Jesus, if only we entrust ourselves to it. See, Leo, here we are now like the penitent thief in Luke's Gospel. He is not delivered by a miracle from his deserved punishment. There on the cross, he learns to own up to his guilt and takes his punishment as the needed purgative. He only pleads to the future king, hanging there beside him, the innocent for the guilty, that he be remembered. 'Today,' says the Lord, 'you will be with me in paradise.'"

"Yes," Leo signed, "but we are in purgatory! If only I could be certain of this. A thousand years are but a day in the Lord's sight. Today? How long must we languish here?"

"It seems to me," Martin replied, "that we have a work to do, a work of grief and truth and reconciliation. The time will fly, if we work at it. And the only pain we must own is the pain of coming into the truth, as light hurts the eyes of one suddenly awoken by its shining in the darkness. It is a grief, a work of grief, to finish out repentance, but a blessed one."

A "blessed grief work," Leo thought, another one of his paradoxes!

MEMORY RANSACKED: LUTHER

I n the state of cognitive dissonance that Luther found himself—the inconsequence of consoling and exhorting the antichrist to the patient work of repentance struck him only moments after the words had fallen from his lips—it was necessary to ransack memory. In truth he had learned this way of self-examination years ago, in his youth as a monk, in reading and rereading the *Confessions* of Augustine; self-knowledge thus gained was precious even if acquired step by painful step in a long exercise before God. So Luther himself formulated in the first of his Ninety-Five Theses: "When our Lord and Master Jesus Christ said, 'Do penance,' he meant for the entire life of the Christian to be one of repentance."

The Ninety-Five Theses argued that purgatory was not to be delayed to another life, let alone short-circuited by the purchase of exemptions from its spiritual pains. In the light of this summons, he came to regard the whole controversy about indulgences as child's play. It had been easily refuted by putting its hawkers on those horns of the dilemma. If purgatory, on the one hand, was intended as punishment to satisfy divine justice, and if the pope really had the power to pardon and release souls from the pains of purgatory, he ought to do so for free out of Christian love. If purgatory was intended for purification of sinful desire, on the other hand, no true Christian would want indulgences but rather would want cross-bearing to gain freedom from sinful desire. His message was thus a prophetic summons, "Purgatory without delay! Purgatory now!" And so he had lived. At least, so he thought. It was now evident, however, that some business had gone unfinished. He was still on the road and had not yet arrived.

It was clear to Luther that Leo knew something of his case by the reference he had made to the "documentation" about it. But Luther wondered if Leo had actually read his condemned writings to determine their sense for himself. He remained suspicious that Leo had relied on summaries prepared by local German enemies like Tetzel or Johannes Eck, a more significant theologian with whom he had debated in Leibzig. Eck was the one who first drew out of Luther the infamous admission that churches, councils, and popes can err. Together with other German papists, Johannes Eck in time created a monstrous image of Martin Luther as a morally derelict and diabolically inspired opponent of all Christian authority and tradition. Such malicious caricatures of Luther's person that smothered knowledge of his teaching determined the Roman Catholic perception of the Reformer for the future.[1]

Yet Luther had risen above those local polemics to write a respectful open letter to Leo with which he prefaced his highly regarded and in some ways programmatic essay, *Freedom of the Christian*.[2] In this way, he had hoped to penetrate the wall—of ignorance, as he supposed—surrounding Leo, erected and maintained by the curia. In the letter he notably appealed to a fellow Renaissance humanist of good moral repute. Had Leo read it?

In fact Leo relied only upon the list of some forty supposedly "heretical" propositions that had been lifted from Luther's writings by his papist opponents in Germany; Luther's suspicion about this was no paranoid fantasy. A memorandum stemming from Eck listing Luther's allegedly heretical assertions—mixed up with ideas of other dissenters—ultimately formed the basis for the papal "bull of excommunication," the official indictment of Luther's false teaching.[3] Upon receipt, the source-critical Luther could read between the lines to see Eck's penmanship in the shadows. He then ceremoniously committed the bull to the flames, to which the bull would eventually condemn him.[4]

26

Memory must be ransacked because memory is fallible. Memory is fallible because, even in the present, attention is selective. Things come into focus for sight as also for understanding only when we exclude the practical infinity of information bombarding us at any moment to attend to what is of concern. What concerns us, moreover, is a matter of interest, taste, and experience, a collage formed daily from birth to death. There is at work in all human acquisition of knowledge, then, a pre-articulate emotional intelligence of desire, roughly sorting the infinity of data for things that matter to us, quickly classified into categories of good and bad, attractive or repulsive, useful or a hindrance. Humans in this way learn progressively and cumulatively through time to sort information; in a feedback loop, the accumulating fund of experiential learning in the world in turn inclines the learner proactively to take interest in this or that, be it threatening danger or promising reward. There is nothing wrong with this embodied way of attending to matters of concern to organic beings; truth be told, it is the only conceivable beginning of knowledge for creatures such as humans are. They remain bound to this beginning even at the heights of the articulate and impersonal knowledge we deem "theoretical" or "scientific." If a child had to learn through rational adult instruction or impersonal observation not to stick his or her finger in the flame, he or she would be roasted body and soul before aversion from fire became second nature to him or her.

This bodily finitude of emotionally formed human perspective that attends, and so learns, only becomes problematic when anyone's process of framing information prematurely closes and becomes absolutized. Then the closed mind acts as if one's vision or understanding was comprehensive and incorrigible, a simple, pure representation of how things are or what is the case. The resulting closed mind can be social and collective, a smothering cultural wet blanket thrown over intellectual curiosity, tabooing new experience and new thoughts. The dogmas of common sense, so called, or tradition are often just that: dogmas that foreclose rather than open up experience to insight. Common sense (if we are "empiricists") or tradition (if we are "historicists") is as often as not "herd mentality" or "group think."

27

Fixed ideas of tradition or naïve representations taken as common sense can blind us to new experience. In this regard a hermeneutics—that is, an interpretive method—of *suspicion* is called for that asks *cui bono* (who benefits?) about common notions apparently settled as if fact. A genealogical investigation then reveals the historicity of what is represented as timelessly adequate to reality, and so it makes commonly accepted matters from yesterday questionable again today. Luther, of course, did not read Nietzsche. Yet the connection is real. The truth is the opposite. Nietzsche, the *real* self-proclaimed "antichrist," at least in this respect, inherited the hermeneutic of suspicion from his Lutheran Christian tradition.[5]

In preparation for writing the Ninety-Five Theses, Luther dove into the annals of canon law to uncover the origin of indulgences and wrote a genealogical account of it. What he discovered there amazed him and his contemporaries. In the earliest stage of church history when Christians were persecuted by the empire, the church had developed a disciplinary procedure for reconciling lapsed Christians after persecution passed. Christians, especially clergy, who had renounced Christ under threat of death to save their lives or to avoid arrest and delivered the Holy Scriptures for destruction into the hands of police, now wanted restoration to the communion. Recognizing the infinitude of divine mercy and the possibility of redemption in the notable figures of Peter who denied Christ and Paul who persecuted Him, the church nevertheless also had the responsibility to test for sincerity of repentance before restoration to communion was granted. Before readmitting the lapsed to communion, church discipline imposed tests for genuine or "godly" sorrow (cf. 2 Cor 7:10) over *sin* (*not* over *punishment*). So the church imposed penalties to test for true faith in forgiveness of sin as a divine gift of mercy. The test consisted in reparative works such as almsgiving. Yet the penance, as a church-imposed penalty, could also be relaxed by the church if and when convinced of the sincerity of the penitent. In that case, the church *indulged* the penitent by suspending continuation of the disciplinary punishment.[6] This relaxation of church imposed penalties to restore the fallen in this life to ecclesial communion, subsequent to demonstration of sincerity by works of reparation, was the ancient origin of the practice of indulgences in Luther's day.

The church's early disciplinary practice of indulgences evolved over the course of many centuries. What began as a measure to restore one to ecclesiastical communion from the special sin of apostasy in this life—the Letter to the Hebrews 6:4-6 seemed to deny even the possibility of restoration!—became generalized and thus torn from its specific context, which was then forgotten. It gradually came to deal with the satisfaction due to the divine and eternal justice for all sins, forgiven but not yet punished, in the next life. So the notion of purgatory as punitive satisfaction of divine justice grew in tandem with the notion of indulgences. Out of the traditional test for sincerity by deeds that repair the injury done, almsgiving evolved into the payment made for the indulgence. Indulgences could now be bought and sold, even if the fiction that they were donations was still maintained. With this excavation of the origins of the sale of indulgences up to his own time, Luther was a pioneer in the genealogical hermeneutic of suspicion (which he had either learned from or found confirmed in the corresponding work of the Italian humanist Lorenzo Valla, who exposed as forgery the document *The Donation of Constantine*, which purportedly had the Roman emperor granting temporal jurisdiction to the bishop of Rome).

There is, however, yet another way in which knowledge becomes fixed and thus immune from the salutary self-questioning that befits human knowing in the perplexities of social life though the changes and chances of life. This happens when one segregates and is never challenged in experience with others to see the same things from different perspectives or to focus empathetically on common matters with the concerns of others. A *hermeneutics of charity*, for which St. Thomas is justly celebrated, learns to love the neighbor as oneself cognitively, by imaginatively seeing things from another's perspective. It affirms as a rule: "Do not presume to criticize until you have stated the opposing position with such precision and empathy that the opponent would exclaim, 'That's it! I couldn't have said it better myself!'" Then, and only then, may critique proceed, for then, and only then, is one dealing with the real thing, not a convenient caricature.

29

When human beings stop learning this most basic social level of fellow-feeling, imagination fails, curiosity dies, and neighbors become nothing but manipulated objects, whether of desire or of aversion, in a vision that only sees but no longer listens, taking its own feelings absolutely as fixed and finished. The question, "Do you see what I see?" never gets asked about the same thing in a conversation, which will not quit until satisfied in common vision, rejoicing with the other in the truth: "Love is patient, love is kind, it isn't jealous, it doesn't brag, it isn't arrogant, it isn't rude, it doesn't seek its own advantage, it isn't irritable, it doesn't keep a record of complaints, it isn't happy with injustice, but it is happy with the truth. Love puts up with all things, trusts in all things, hopes for all things, endures all things" (1 Cor 13:4-7). Consequently a hermeneutic of suspicion, unchecked by the hermeneutic of charity, succumbs to the injurious fallacy of a collective ad hominem, demonizing those who see differently as if herds or, rather in Luther's case, "hordes" of devils.

This failure in charity, alas, was Luther's peculiar self-indulgence in the polemical caricatures of papists, peasants, and Jews (to name only the most significant victims of his impatient wrath), at which he excelled in his verbally violent culture.[7] This failure in charity, moreover, dogged Luther's rediscovery of the biblical gospel, when at times it descended into an equal and opposite hermeneutic of authoritarianism and obscurantism: Luther's miraculous Bible against the church's miraculous pope. In this dive into the gutter, "proof-texting" prevails, which settles arguments with citations from authorities like a trump card. Unnoticed in the process is the selective focus on certain statements, ignoring others, without any account to the other of who it is who finds such statements significant and why and whether their selection can be justified in view of the whole range of possible selections. Proof-texting thus imposes in authoritarian fashion a tacit and unwarranted selection from the body of evidence without the bother of learning what the selected statements were intended to mean from the speaker/writer's perspective, or how they hang together with the canonical whole; instead proof-texts are weaponized from the perspective of one's own absolutized and unchecked will-to-power.

On account of these not insignificant failures in love, Luther now found himself in purgatory. So he came to see, as he ransacked memory before God, as God had placed him together with his enemy in the ante-room of heaven. There was thus much more to ponder.

To be sure, as he who loved the disputation reflected, at its rarified best proof-texting seeks to bracket out human subjectivity entirely with its prejudices and confirmation biases and to attend with logical rigor to selected propositions to test their claims to truth objectively. This virtue is real in medieval scholastic procedures of disputation, in which any and all arguments were abstracted from their human proponents and social contexts in the world and evaluated scientifically on their own proposi-tional terms, as it seemed, by testing logic and probing evidence. Yet even in treating another's statements as propositions making claims to truth, one has already, though subtly, predestined interpretation. For the state-ments found in language are rarely pure claims to truth suitable for such abstracted treatment and argumentation. Discovering what is an origi-nal and thus originating claim to truth is a prior and difficult exercise of mind. Luther spoke of this as the priority of grammar over dialectic,[8] or, in today's language, of rhetorical analysis over logical analysis.

Indeed, the claim to truth that anyone makes is often not evident, even to its author who, like every embodied creature, is swimming in a river of constant change, struggling for clarity, venturing ideas for their workability more than making leisured propositions. Here a claim to truth emerges, even for its author, as the laborious product of patient listening, experiential testing and protracted dialogue, presupposing a society of in-terpretation characterized by goodwill, curiosity, and imagination as well as common purposes, logical rigor, and attention to evidence, especially negative evidence that seems disconfirming of working hypotheses. In this dialogical process of an extended, socially embodied *argument* (Alis-dair MacIntyre's better understanding of what "tradition" actually is[9]), a hermeneutics of charity is indispensable.

If this situatedness in the struggle to love is the situation of hu-man claims to knowledge in Christianity, language as the discourse of generation-spanning communities united by circumstances is the universal,

31

albeit irreducibly multiple inheritance (since the Tower of Babel! [Gen 11:1-9]), which makes dispute about truth possible in the first place. In that case, rhetorical analysis precedes logical argument, "grammar" before "dialectic." One must understand the genre, the form of language in its form of life, from which a proposition emerges to grasp its actual sense as a claim to truth. Consequently, it is authoritarian abuse of others to say theologically, "God said it. I believe it. That settles it!" Perhaps it is so, but the intervening questions are, "Do you understand it?" "Can you give good reasons for your understanding to others?" "Is God actually speaking here to you?" In one respect, then, it was just this authoritarian method of interpretation that privileged (selected) texts at the expense of context, and logic at the expense of rhetoric, from which Renaissance humanism had broken free, Luther included, and, as he might have expected early on, the Medici from Florence and fellow humanist who had been elected pope.

Understanding how medieval scholasticism concealed this hidden authoritarianism requires further genealogy.[10] More than three centuries before Peter Lombard had created the basic textbook for theology in the medieval universities that institutionalized the "scholastic" method of reconciling the apparent contradictions found between authoritative statements taken from the Bible and the church fathers. One might well wonder just why this question of apparent contradiction in authoritative texts had arisen at just this juncture. Lombard, in any case, compiled series of propositions from these sources and grouped them under broad categories to unveil the apparent contradictions. The working assumption was that the statements were to be received on authority as true. The problem—created not least by tearing the statements from literary context and treating these abstracted selections as pure propositions—was that these many statements had now to be reconciled, if truth is to be one and have the actual force of sacred authority for us. A "master of the sentences," as one who had mastered Lombard's textbook, had to show logical prowess in reconciling the apparent contradictions of these authoritative statements. Virtuosity in theology consisted in harmonizing the authorities by the logical arts of making distinctions and drawing inferences and probing the validity of evidence. Both Luther and Leo has been educated in this fashion. Neither, be it well noted, despised the logical prowess this procedure had produced in these centuries.

Turning now to the question of why the problem had arisen at this juncture, the turn from the so-called Dark Ages to the Middle Ages. This new theological method of the "schools" (hence, "scholastic" or less pejoratively, "scholarly," "academic," or even "scientific" theology) marked a transition from the previous home of theological reflection in the monasteries to the newly founded universities in Europe. Yet by the time of Luther and Leo, it had also become sterile, as the procedure had multiplied schools of thought seemingly engaged in endless "logic-chopping" disputation about increasingly abstract subtleties. The root assumptions and motives from the origins of scholasticism were not thus forgotten; they were actually betrayed. Despite the common name, there was no unified scholastic theology in the doctrinal sense at all. Rather than reconciling the contradictions in the authoritative statements, the plurality of rival schools seemed instead to reproduce and even accentuate them.

But why, in the first place, be concerned with the inconsistencies found between verses of the Bible or from statements of the fathers? As Ernst Käsemann once pointed out, the Bible is not the source of the unity of the church but rather of its multiplicity.[11] So we casually speak of about Petrine Catholicism or Pauline Lutheranism or Johannine Eastern Orthodoxy. Thus, even though all agreed on the authoritative texts as such, there was in fact little doctrinal unity in scholasticism between Dominicans and Franciscans, realists and nominalists, papists and conciliarists, analogists and univocalists, sacramental symbolists and sacramental realists, and so on. But why should this theological pluralism disturb us? It would disturb only if it reflects a failure of the root intention of the scholastic method going back to its origins in Lombard's program. Scholasticism, as noted, did not succeed in reconciling the authorities but rather reproduced in its various schools the variety of positions found in the authoritative texts—an unreconciled disunity that can be held together not by theological argument (which reinforces it) but instead by sacralizing institutional power. So it was that more and more the papacy refereed the scholastic arguments and enforced limits on disputation. But was this new solution a theological success or a profound failure in the original mission of scholastic theology?

Luther was not satisfied with this kind of authoritarian solution. But to grasp this dissatisfaction correctly, we cannot ascribe to Luther the genesis of what later came to be called "free thinking," surely not in the realm of theology—he whose conscience was *captive* to the word of God! We must rather dig a little deeper. The reason for the futility of scholasticism in this genealogical dig goes back to Lombard's organization of the problem of theology as one of reconciling authorities taken on authority. This procedure, as the humanist movement saw in its reaction against scholastic sterility, actually short-circuited rhetorical analysis of what the excerpted statements from the Bible and the fathers might have meant in their original contexts. *Ad fontes! To the sources!* That was the humanist slogan in the sense that rhetorical analysis of the originating documents had to come first in academic procedure. For surely it was the original meaning of the word of God that ought to organize the inquiry of theology, if the church and its mission in the world is continuously generated as the *creatura Verbi*, the creature of the divine Word, ever summoned into its existence and enlightened to its purpose by the sounding of that generative Word. That insight will lead not to a futile attempt to reconcile every foolish thing whether said in the Bible or by the church fathers but to the authority of a specific word of God, *the gospel*, to author and authorize a particular mission and vocation in the world in distinction from misconstructions or deviations that subvert or confuse that gospel mission and vocation. Luther put this crucial point in this way in the *Freedom of the Christian*:

> You may ask, "What then is the Word of God, and how shall it be used, since there are so many words of God?" I answer: The Apostle explains this in Romans 1. The Word is the gospel of God concerning his Son, who was made flesh, suffered, rose from the dead, and was glorified through the Spirit who sanctifies. To preach Christ means to feed the soul, make it righteous, set it free, and save it, provided it believes the preaching. Faith alone is the saving and efficacious use of the Word of God, according to Rom. 10[:9]: "If you confess with your lips that Jesus is Lord and believe in your

heart that God raised him from the dead, you will be saved." Furthermore, "Christ is the end of the law, that every one who has faith may be justified" [Rom 10:4]. Again, in Rom. 1[:17], "He who through faith is righteous shall live." The Word of God cannot be received and cherished by any works whatever but only by faith. Therefore it is clear that, as the soul needs only the Word of God for its life and righteousness, so it is justified by faith alone and not any works; for if it could be justified by anything else, it would not need the Word, and consequently it would not need faith.[12]

In this retrospective light, the forgotten or suppressed problem at the origins of scholasticism was the crisis of authority brought on by the Western Christian breach with Byzantium, the anomaly of living Judaism within its Christendom, and the encroachment of Islam from outside. All these opponents in various ways called attention to the "many words of God," that is, the contradictions in the sources that Western Christianity since Charlemagne had claimed to sanctify its civilizational project. There were many and varied words of God urgently requiring scholarly harmonization, lest the enemies of the church scoff at the absurdities and contradictions of Latin Christianity. Under intellectual pressure from the outside in Islam, and from Judaism within Christendom, and from the rupture with Eastern Christianity, there was thus a tacitly apologetic intention at work in the root assumptions and motives of scholastic theology. This apologetic orientation may be seen in Anselm's method of arguing *solo ratione*, by reason alone, to overcome the habitual, knee-jerk proof-texting which could have no cognitive traction with critics outside the parochial community of the West and its monasteries. It may likewise be seen in Thomas Aquinas's celebrated *Summary of the Faith against the Gentiles*, that is, against the Jews and the Muslims (and the ancient pagan philosophers whom they claimed for their unitarian theologies) over and against the great Christian absurdities of incarnation and Trinity.

Given this root motive and intention to argue by reason alone in such fashion as to defend the Christian mysteries from the accusation of absurdity by philosophy, Judaism, and Islam, the scholastic solution proved self-defeating in producing the contending schools, more and more remote from the originating gospel that had first produced the dogmas of incarnation and Trinity. Indeed, the apologetic intention inevitably causes the tail to wag the dog. It allowed if not encouraged reliance on extraneous structures of thought to organize the information of theology. For no apology for faith can prevail against opponents except on some common ground extraneous to the controverted claim. The churchly ground of Scripture and tradition, however, was precisely what could not be held in common with ancient Greek philosophers, Jews, and Muslims; the New Testament content of incarnation and Trinity was precisely what these others refused a priori as absurd on allegedly common rational grounds. So another basis for argumentation had to be sought, if the defense of Christianity was to have rational traction.

Most notably, as Luther had come to see, that common ground in scholasticism was a theological idea that can be traced back to the pre-Christian philosopher of imperial Greece. For Aristotle, God was God as perfectly thinking God in serene rapture, like a mind contemplating its own perfection, incapable of disruption and timelessly eternal.[13] "God" was the perfect intellectual being who inspired and captured human desire. Wouldn't it be *great* to be like God, blissfully and totally self-aware, never troubled or tempted by other or lesser or evil beings? With this supposedly neutral or common ground of the philosophical notion of perfect being eliciting desire and structuring the organization of theological knowledge, theology became an articulation of the human quest for "beatitude," as Aristotle's notion of happiness was Christianized. Within this common desire for perfect being, Christian theology could claim to be the authoritatively revealed religion that provided the certain road to the blissful vision. Christ is, as Thomas Aquinas accordingly held, "man's road to God." So Christianity can be harmonized internally and vindicated against the criticisms of its enemies. Jew, Muslims, and Greek philosophers could, as humans created in God's image, arise to the notion of true deity in thought, but they had no way to arise there in reality. What they disdain as Christian contradiction is in fact this way, truth, and life given as a gracious gift.

Failing such syntheses of philosophical generality and Christian particularity—and since the time of Thomas Aquinas, his own and subsequent attempts of others after him at such syntheses failed to achieve the hoped-for rational consensus—all that would remain to keep the theological project of Christendom intact was the external discipline of papal authority. The attempted syntheses were doomed to failure, Luther came to argue, because what the gospel means by "God" and what "perfect being ontotheology" (as we call it since Heidegger) means by God are just not the same thing. As Luther famously put it in the 1518 Heidelberg Disputation, for the philosophers, "the object of love is its cause," (i.e., His perfection inspires creatures to seek in God their highest good). But "this is the love of the cross, born of the cross, which turns in the direction in which it does not find a good that it may enjoy, but where it may confer a good on a bad or needy person." The God of the gospel does not find but creates the object of His love.[14]

St. Thomas, to be sure, can write beautifully of the creative love of God: it "belongs properly to the nature of love that the lover will the good of the one he loves. Now, God wills His own good and that of others.... This means, therefore that God loves Himself and other things."[15] Here love is an essential quality like Luther had been thinking of Paul's "righteousness." Thomas shows how this divine quality is proper to God, though not as a passion like in creatures. As proper to God, the love of God means that God wills the proper good of each creature and that all things in turn are joined to God as the source of all goodness, "which all things imitate."[16] "There is, therefore, in God not only a true, but also a most perfect and a most enduring love."[17] It is further proper to love "to move towards union" as in the "privilege of friends to take joy in one another's presence, in living together, and in conversation."[18] So God moves all things to such union with Himself and one another. Union excludes exclusion. Nothing exists properly in God "save joy and love."[19] So when Scripture speaks of God's anger or punishment, it is not speaking properly but only metaphorically. This sets aside the "error of certain Jews who attributed anger, sadness, repentance, and all such passions in their proper sense to God, failing to distinguish what in Scripture is said properly and what metaphorically."[20] Luther would be in Thomas's mind such a Jewish errorist.[21]

Notice, all that Thomas has said is said to be true by nature; thus God's love is most perfect and most enduring. By contrast, creation as a special temporal act of God as depicted in the book of Genesis (not to mention incarnation or new creation) could not be properly attributed to God. It must be taken as a pictorial representation of God's eternal love for Himself and others. Since this is a most difficult reading of Genesis, Thomas in fact could only accept a beginning of creation as a supernatural truth of revelation beyond reason, since the notion of perfect being did not and could not admit that God, being perfect, could ever initiate anything new. Novelty would signify divine imperfection, the lack of something not yet existent, a possibility not yet actualized. But God's eternal love is simply nothing new.

For Luther, Thomas's appeal here to supernatural revelation only masked the underlying problem of incompatible theologies in his sources; in the passage on God's eternally creative love, the Neoplatonist Dionysius is the authority Thomas draws upon. Sometime later, Duns Scotus saw better that the Christian doctrine of God "who makes all things new" included the free creation of a world other than God, but this led him to the idea, not countenanced by Thomas, that free creatures could, as it were, bootstrap themselves up to the perfect being by their own enlightened act of will, which God would naturally reward. So the radical human need for grace was undermined in Scotus just like the radical freedom of God to create was undermined in Thomas.

One could go on. Not by accident, the procedure of academic theology with its generation of multiple schools subverted its own founding intention of rational unification of Christendom in doctrine defended and vindicated against Jewish, Muslim, and philosophical critiques. The papacy more and more emerged as the final court of appeal when and if theological disputes about the meaning of the authoritative writings threatened unity. It was, in hindsight, only natural that Luther's theological challenge would be met and defeated, not on its own merits of articulating the gospel's originating power and Scripture's normative witness to it, but on the grounds that in the process he subverted the one doctrine

and practice that actually held Christendom together against its enemies: the papacy.

Luther's so-called Reformation "breakthrough" was nothing if not a resolution to the tacit dispute about the accepted meaning of authoritative writings as authoritative simply because supposedly revealed, the determination of their sense being a secondary matter epistemically. In his emergent humanist view, the peculiar nature of the word of God named "gospel" was being systematically misread in scholasticisms of every stripe in the mere fact of being treated this way as authoritative as such. This construction puts the gospel on the same level as any other writing putatively revealing divine order on the common sense assumption that religion is about monotheism and morality. But for Luther the gospel is revealed because it is something good and new in the world that is reducing "what is considered to be something to nothing" (1 Cor 1:28). It is not gospel just because it is, that is, claims to be revealed. Or, to put the matter doctrinally, the doctrine of the incarnation is a reflex of the primitive kerygma of the resurrection of the crucified Jesus. It is not in the order of theological knowing that the Incarnate One happened to be crucified and raised, but that the Crucified One whom God exalted and vindicated was thus revealed as the Incarnate Son.

A hidden challenge from Islam was at work here. Though it was beyond Luther's historical grasp to fully realize this, he was indeed highly skeptical of the renewed crusade ideology issuing from Leo's office. Even more deeply, he had with his thoughts about the word of God that authors and authorizes the church as the mission of the gospel penetrated to the root critique Islam had made of Christianity at its own origins in the "recitations" the prophet Mohammed made in listening to the divine word: namely, that instead of purely reciting the simple message of Islam as submission to God's will first given to Abraham, the Christians, like the Jews, had perverted this simple message of submission by adding their human thoughts to it. And these additions, blasphemously, were, in the case of Judaism, that Israel is God's chosen people and light to the nations, and, in the case of Christianity, that Jesus is God's chosen One, more than a messenger of monotheism and morality, but rather the Incarnate Son of God and savior of the world. This challenge of Islam to Christianity had provoked the scholastic strategy, so to say, of meeting reason with reason, authority with authority, revelation with revelation, inspired text with inspired text. But for Luther this entire strategy was systematically misleading in the sense that it led away from the particular message of the Christian canonical texts. This "gospel" of the paradoxical predication "Christ crucified" was precisely not a pure and simple claim to authority as religiously understood, but rather for a "*new* teaching with authority" (Mark 1:27) in the sense of a *saving* authority coming on the scene to silence demons and forgive sins and give life to the dead.

All this discovery of Luther as he worked past the then prevalent rivalries in authoritarianism could be captured in the insight that in the Bible the term *righteousness of God* is not meant in the way that lawyers and philosophers conceive, as God's moral quality by means of which a perfect being as such imposes order on the chaos beneath. Rather, it is meant in the "Hebrew way," as Luther put it, of God giving as a saving gift the righteousness that counts before Him to and for the sake of those otherwise weak, ungodly, even "enemies." It was God's saving righteousness manifest, not as the quiescent quality of a perfect being in perfect repose, but in the obedience of Jesus to death on a cross for the sake of those lesser and undeserving.[22]

Not accidentally in reading righteousness "in the Scriptural way," Luther's breakthrough came about as a result of his break from scholastic method and his adoption of the "humanist" method of the Renaissance[23]; the designation of "humanist" does *not* mean humanocentric in substance, like a turn in orientation away from God or the cosmos to humanity and the existential questions of individuals. Rather, it designates an alternative method of study that recognizes the primacy of language in human science and thus attends to "grammar" (rhetoric) before "dialectic" (logic). It was studying the usage of Scripture and setting aside the preconceived ideas of lawyers and philosophers that led Luther to his breakthrough. While it may be that "God is not a story" (Francesca Murphy) in the sense of a fable made up by creatures, the God of the gospel, as the living God, is capable of story in sharing His *life* with creatures and indeed writes Himself into their story and also writes their stories into His. And this consummate being of God in the fulfillment of His promises is God everlasting, who cries in triumph, "Look! I'm making all things new!" (Rev 21:5).

Many contemporary humanists, especially in Italian Florence from which Leo came, saw in Plato's literary style a corresponding alternative to the dry argumentation of the schools under the influence of Aristotle; to justify this literary aesthetic, they appealed to the Platonic assumption that human reason is not an abstract mind doing calculations like a thinking machine but a sublime form of desire, embodied then in a creature who is in all things seeking its good. For Luther the holistic truism of humanism that all seek the good, however, was qualified by deep drinking at the well of St. Augustine, a pioneer in the tradition of Christian Platonism at the fonts of Western civilization, who taught that, fallen into sin, corrupt creatures seek their goods so corruptly that the goods they seek, seen corruptly and used corruptly, become idols that fail or demons that enslave.

Augustine had famously stipulated that the human heart is restless until it rests in the One who is truly God, the very Creator of all that is not God, which is what Luther means with the phrase "the one, true God." But Augustine in the very same passage from the beginning of his *Confessions* immediately went on to attribute this restlessness to the word of God, which is at work to de-secure the self-satisfied self.[24] "Which comes first—to call upon you or to praise you[...?] But who calls upon you when he does not know you...? You have been preached to us. My faith, Lord, calls upon you. It is your gift to me. You breathed it into me by the humanity of your Son, by the ministry of your preacher."[25] This Augustinianism gave a sharp critical edge to Luther's humanism, even militating against the Platonist alternative to Aristotle so popular in Leo's Florence by the sharp line drawn between Creator and creature: not any goods are the one and true God. Mostly, they are idols behind which demons lurk. This is especially true about enticing intellectual goods bought at the expense of bodily renunciation, as old and new Platonists taught.

Lacking revelation, as Augustine had seen, the Platonist cannot but dualize human beings into mind, seeking the ideas that tell the Good

41

above, at war with body, distracted by earthly fears and pleasures. Superficially similar to the Pauline warfare of the Spirit against the flesh, this anthropological dualism of Platonism permutated anew in Renaissance humanism and continued on in the passage to Enlightenment philosophy, reappearing particularly in Descartes and Kant.[26] But for Luther following Augustine following Paul, the Spirit is not human mind but the divine Spirit of the Father of the Lord Jesus who comes upon the self-bound self to teach it trust, no longer in its own brain power or muscle power, but in the invisible things promised by the word of God. The battle line then is drawn, not between animal body and intellectual soul, but between a human world of corrupted desire, *amor concupiscentiae*, seeking self in all things (as Luther put it), on one side, and a new creation in which God becomes all things to everyone, on the other. The former is "flesh" in the sense of human self-reliance and the latter is Spirit in the sense of reliance on the promise of the "one, true God."

This notion of the "one, true God" might easily be misunderstood today as an assertion of religious superiority, as if our tribal deity were the true one and all the others false. It requires careful examination and appreciation of Luther's bedrock Augustinianism to understand that Luther has something else entirely in mind; indeed, he is trying with the notion of the "one, true God" to get past the tribal warfare of the gods. Just as the prophets of Israel matured to the teaching that God can judge His own people when they turn God into a national idol (cf. Amos 3:2), Luther pits the "one, true God" against the idols manufactured in the religion business for chauvinistic purposes. As he once said, if we believed the "one, true God" it would hardly confirm us in our sense of religiously sanctioned nationalistic superiority to others. It would rather "terrify us."[27]

In the same writing on Israel's ten commandments, Luther deleted the historical prologue identifying "the Lord" who speaks the commandments as the saving Lord who had rescued Israel from Egyptian bondage in favor of this "natural law" notion of the "one, true God." The *henotheistic* first commandment of Israel—not to set up the idols of other gods before the empty throne of the ark of the covenant, the seat of the invisible LORD Yahweh in the tabernacle—thus becomes in Luther's Christian rereading (but also in Jewish rereadings as, for example, in the second Isaiah) the command of radical *monotheism*[28] not to fear, love, or trust anyone or anything less than the one and only true God, that is, the *One who is creator of all that is other than God*, unique and incomparable. That is not a Jewish tribal God nor a Christian tribal God, but rather the One who is the creator of all else, of everything that is not God. Only such a Creator of all things "out of nothing" qualifies as the one, true God. This is the God who is the eternal fountain of generosity, who gives without any need of return. This God is the "the one, eternal good," whose gifts may only be received and blessed with thanksgivings that do not separate the gifts from the Giver, but in all things, *soli Deo gloria*, give the glory to God alone.

This notion of the "one, true God" grounds Luther's remarkable exploration into what it means "to have a God," namely, as something more like "being had" or captivated. Whatever captures desire at its seat in the human heart is one's operational deity. To "have" a God, then, is like all kinds of other "having" in that something becomes my own, my very own, in an act of personal appropriation, as in, "He or she becomes my beloved."[29] But to have "God" is not like any other kind of possession in the world of creatures that one could come to dispose over, since the one, true God is not a creature alongside others but the one, true Giver of all creatures. This in turn makes all creatures, including the self, gifts of God to be received with joy and thanksgiving and the kinds of love that variously befit these various gifts.

To have God "the Giver," then, is to fear only God's disapproval, to value or esteem God's approval above all, to trust that God's approval is generous and merciful. To have God is the kind of having that the "heart" has, which can never possess its beloved like a thing to be used, but rather can "have" God in fear, love, and trust above all others. Having God in this way of being had by the One who truly gives all, then, entails loving all creatures in and under God as also gifts from God, just as the second table of the commandments goes on to elaborate. By contrast, then, not having One who is truly God entails makings gods of one's possessions, greedily hording them, and justifying one's greed in the name of rational self-interest. A merely negative civil righteousness, then, which does not visibly trespass the prohibitions can conceal a self that is greed personified. Or, as in Jesus's parable, a "fool" who puts an infinite burden of desire on a finite treasure that cannot but fail. To be sharply drawing the ontological line between the one, true God and all His creatures, Luther has, following Augustine, broken at the decisive point from a kind of Christian Platonism in which the cosmos participates ontologically in God's being through a great chain of being in favor of the eschatological battlefield depicted in biblical narrative between the earthly city and the city of God.

Luther's hero among the Italian humanists was neither of the great Florentine Platonists, Marsilio Facino or Giovanni Pico della Mirandola, in whose orbit Leo has been educated.[30] Rather it was the Augustinian Lorenza Valla, who had first attempted to displace scholastic logic with a rhetorical science in order to focus attention, like Augustine, on the problematic desire that moves creatures in all that they think, do, and say by its formation through language prior to any conscious reflection or choice.[31] For Valla as for Augustine, there is a spiritual conflict between the proud creature who wants to be God and the humble Creator who out of unfathomable love for the sake of this proud and troubled being descends to share its disgrace and to so overcome it with unmerited grace. Adam wants to be God, but the true Son of God wants to be human. For Valla following Augustine, and Luther following both, as God in Christ had descended to the creature in grace, so it is for Adam the disgracing sin of pride—sublimely, intellectual pride—when the creature thinks to ascend in its mind to God, despising the body that God has created and made the object of His redemption. A fitting reward as well—what Adam comes to in this ascent is the idol of thought thinking itself, the dream of transcendence, not the one, true God who shows true deity in incarnation and cross, as the Father of the Son in the Spirit.

The revolutionary import of this line of theological reflection was that sin resides not in the body and its natural, earthly desires, but in the soul, in the mind, in the higher powers of the human creature. As a result, anything other than God can be by made by the mind into a false god, an idol, and so a god that will fail. Gross addictions and emotional obsessions merely illustrate graphically this destructive turn of the inner person, the

44

soul, the mind. But what makes such destructive dives into carnality sinful is that they are and remain *human* dives and *spiritual* turns from the one true God to some other help and healer than "the one, true God."

Thus, for Luther, a humanist in Valla's train and a neo-Augustinian, the task of critical theological thinking was to penetrate and expose the idols that captivate desire and to show forth the liberator who breaks into the strong man's house to plunder his goods by recapturing human desire. The pre-Reformation Luther had so defined the theological task in his 1516 commentary on Romans, "to pull down, to pluck up, and to destroy all wisdom and righteousness of the flesh (i.e., of whatever importance they may be in the sight of men and even in our own eyes) no matter how heartily and sincerely they may be practiced, and to implant, establish, and make large the reality of sin (however unconscious we may be of its existence). Hence, Blessed Augustine says..."[32] Statements of the "blessed Augustine," as we haves seen, were never far from Luther's mind.

Memory must be ransacked because the depth of sin is blissful ignorance of this captivation of desire, which must be uncovered by the Spirit in a genealogy of the soul. True self-awareness comes as a painful theological gift. Natural reason lacks the space that grace creates to come to terms with its own unconscious desires—the proverbial thoughts that would shame hell. Only grace breaks down this castle in the air of human self-transcendence and breaks into this prison house of self-imposed immanence to enable self-knowledge that does not collapse into nihilism's death wish but instead creates trust in the heart and hope for a new future. It is not as if human desire is the innocent power, as Nietzsche imagined, latent in any individual able to bootstrap its own liberation from the fetters of tradition and society by creating its own language, as also romantic interpreters of Luther beginning with Herder have thought. Such a private language would be, in any case, a contradiction in terms; language is social all the way down. Just so, as soon as infants hear and speak, desire is always already being captured by the very language in which it is articulated. Desire then can only be liberated by new language articulating new loves. Such saving work belongs to the particular "word of God," which is the "gospel" in the mode of its theological creativity in constructing a new and theological language.[33]

From infancy human desire is formed socially by language, which is always a particular, historically conditioned, and so also historically mutable system of signs that enables reasoning of and about desire and its objects in the first place.[34] Language is thus far more than a neutral conveyer belt for information that reason objectively processes. Language is performative before it is informative. Mommy teaches us what is yucky and what is yummy before we have any say in the matter. As the inheritance of valuations—that is to say, of loves of the heart—internalized from the cooing or frowning enunciations of parents onward, language forms the heart's desires before one ever knows anything articulately; language indoctrinates the heart with likes and dislikes, instilling "emotional intelligence" (or "stupidity," in the case of incompetent or absent parents). This ineradicable matrix of language is both a continuously creative work and at the same time the inheritance of sin encoding false antitheses, misleading tropes, and built-in barriers to boot against those who speak another language. Not race or racial ethnicity, but the tale of the Tower of Babel (Gen 11:1-9), defines this human predicament for Luther and fellow humanists. Learning other languages, then, as the foundation for the cultural inquiries of the *studia humanitatis* becomes for the humanists a veritable instruction in this human condition.

Such were Luther's Greek and Hebrew studies: endeavors summoned by humanism's turn *ad fontes*, "to the sources," that is, away from the much-muddied downstream waters of ecclesiastical tradition to the pure source of the stream in the Scriptures. Here, especially in the Hebrew Scriptures, Luther found much reinforcement for his humanist convictions in Valla's Augustinian train. He found there that the "heart" (rather than the "head") is the seat of human personhood. Whoever captures the heart captures the whole person, the head obediently following. Thus Luther's Hebrew studies also taught him that the heart with its desires articulates as faith in the sense of trust. That to which the heart clings in every time of trouble is really its god. The question is not whether we trust in

46

something greater than ourselves. Inevitably we do. The question is what is worthy of all our trust.

The notion of the "one, true God" as the only One worthy of all trust arose, as mentioned, not as a totalizing claim for a particular religion, but rather as the recognition that only the One who is truly Creator of everything that is not God can be invested with all our trust. Who this one, true God is—that is, how this one, true God is to be known and recognized—is, however, a question of particular revelations, more precisely, *self*-revelations putatively giving this identification of God as a gift from God! There is a circle here, but it is virtuous not vicious. It is virtuous because the point is not to establish a rational foundation of human certainty (Luther is quite skeptical that such could ever be found; rational life confines us to truisms or probabilities). The point is rather the *certainty of faith*—another of Luther's *paradoxes*—indicating faith that can *rest* its restless heart in Another so that it can be active for others in the same love discovered in that Other.

So Luther explained:

> They are perfect who return to God whatever they owe, because they owe nothing more than the offering of their total selves along with their inmost will. God requires of man nothing more than his total self, as he says: "My son, give me your heart" [Prov 23:26].... Is God so cruel that the soul which thirsts for him with the greatest love, and loves him most fervently above everything else, which has fully forgiven its neighbor all things, and desires most fervently that it itself may be forgiven all things, which because of these things has deserved forgiveness before God and men (for such is the soul of one who dies with pure love), here, I say, is God so cruel that he does not remit...?[35]

Such faith in the glory of God displayed in free grace, even while not yet perfected, justifies because it believes the word of Christ proclaiming this God.[36] That objectivity of faith is its certainty, which is the only certainty yet available.

Desire is never fully satisfied and can never be fully satisfied so long as a creature lives. The extinction of desire would be, rather, death; so the satisfaction of desire, as opposed to its extinction in frustration, would be to love a kind of life that triumphs over death. The kind of peace or satisfaction that restless human desire can rest in already here and now on the earth, then, does not consist in building bigger barns or cultivating private gardens, let alone conquering other peoples or subjugating nature. It is a matter of entrusting oneself to Another whose word promises care and whose care is and can be thought to be reliable and wise. Faith is such personal knowledge, such emotional intelligence, such articulate trust or trusting belief. So the just will live in an unjust world by their faith, as the prophet Habakkuk taught, just as the unjust person lives by false trust in false gods.

Thus God becomes the object of faith's knowledge. One trusts the One in whom one comes to believe and one believes this One so far as one understands this One. Although some later followers of Luther have argued—more like Tertullian than Luther—that trust is blind, ignorant of its object, absurd in the world, and a leap in the dark, they misunderstand Luther at this crucial point. In their justified desire to reject an ideal of knowledge as gazing contemplation, which comprehends and in this sense makes God into an object like other objects in the world, they miss the pragmatic knowledge of God on which trust depends to trust at all. The one who cannot identify whom she trusts can and will consequently trust anything and anyone, and so there would be no difference between faith and idolatry, conviction and fanaticism, love of God and captivation by the demons. "Thus everything must be read and accepted with fear and judgment, even that which is handed down by great and holy men," Luther writes, citing 1 Thessalonians 5:21 and 1 John 4:1.[37] The one who trusts in God knows the One who is believed. One believes in order to understand and one understands in order to believe.

This is possible, Luther realized, in developing Augustine's theory of signs because as Augustine rightly saw in philosophy (that is, in worldly knowledge of objects), the sign represents the absence, not the presence, of the thing signified. That is the brilliance and power of language, through words that bring to mind the vast repertoire of things in the world not at the moment present to sight or touch or hearing. It is also the poverty of language, however, that indicates a painful distance between things in the mind and things in the world. In the matter of desire, the sign is no substitute for the thing signified! On the basis of this reflection Augustine had thought of the words of revelation as signs pointing away from themselves to the heavenly things signified as the true objects of desire. Strictly speaking, one does not for Augustine believe in Jesus Christ as an object like other objects in the world, but through the sign, Jesus Christ, to the eternal Word of the Father spoken in eternity. But in theology, Luther thought, unlike philosophy, the sign indicates not the absence but the presence of the thing signified, at least where and when the Spirit wills. If this is so, the mystery of the incarnation attends the creature Jesus Christ, an object dwelling with us like other objects in the world, yet full of grace and truth. Of course, this unification of sign and thing signified is something quite extraordinary; it is, for Luther, the sovereign work and gift of the Spirit and thus perceptible to faith alone.

LUTHER'S BREAKTHROUGH

With such reflections Luther came to his so-called breakthrough. An earnest monk, Luther had come to hate the thought of the "righteousness of God," which, as he read in the Apostle Paul's Letter to the Romans, was "revealed in the gospel." He hated it because, if thinking philosophically of the perfect being, this alleged revelation poured salt into his wounded soul. He was already wounded by the dreadful thought of standing before the perfect being and justifying himself; indeed he hated this being who, he not unfairly reasoned, had set him up with all humanity to fail. Such hatred of the God who created him only to damn him further reinforced his sense of captivated desire doomed to damnation. The scruples learned from his schooling as a monk, coupled with a rare honesty about self and the actual desires of the heart, showed him that he could not will himself, so to speak, to will love of God. Coerced love under the duress of threatened punishment is phony; it is the love of a slave and not of a beloved child. It seeks self in averting punishment or securing reward and so never comes to a free and joyful love of God. If it were not bad enough that God's strict standard of judgment was revealed in the law and the prophets, now Christ himself in the gospel appeared as the righteous judge of the living and the dead coming from heavenly perfection! Christ, the vicar of the perfect being! How will his heart be delivered from its altogether rational hatred of this perfect being to stand before the judgment seat of Christ? How will the perfect ever become lovable to him, created as an imperfect being? Resolution of that quandary is what Luther sought in seeking a "gracious God."

The easy answer would be that in a cathartic experience Luther changed his representation of God from that of a wrathful judge demanding perfection to that of a loving father indulging imperfection. That easy answer would interpret the breakthrough, however, still on the level of Augustine's theory of signs. A better sign of loving-kindness pointing to the thing signified has now replaced the older sign pointing to wrathful vengeance. On that account, the breakthrough would represent merely a change in Luther's consciousness; pushed hard, it would confuse the effect (Luther's new self-understanding) with the cause (the coming of God in grace to the sinner). It is of course true that a change in representation took place for Luther; Luther taught, as we have seen, that "as a person believes so it will be with him"[38] or "it is not the sacrament but faith in the sacrament which justifies."[39] But it was not the new representation that changed Luther or more precisely Luther's relation to God. It was rather—shocking thought to one schooled in the idea of the perfect being knowing and willing itself in timeless and untroubled self-contemplation—God who had changed God, going out from divine bliss to undertake human unblessedness, there to overcome it. By this coming in grace, God is now perceived as the One who would rather be unblessed with us than blessed without us. And so a change in representation resulted. When this *coming* of God to the sinner penetrated his consciousness, Luther broke through to the Pauline meaning of the term *righteousness of God*, not as a quiescent quality of a heavenly substance, but as the saving event of God surpassing God.[40] The "righteousness of God" is latterly revealed in Christ because it was first decided and accomplished in Christ, God's great *innovation* in the divine resolve from eternity to keep with this faithless creature and bring it by the missions of God's very Son to redemption and by God's Spirit to fulfillment.

So a series of unifications of sign and thing signified occurred when God broke through to Luther. God unified the proclamation of the man on the cross with the message of the Lamb who takes away the sin of the world. God unified the troubled sinner with Christ's righteous love. God unified the isolated monk seeking a righteousness of his own with all the helpless sinners of the world. Such divine acts unifying sign and thing signified change the world. It is a *translatio rerum*, "a change of things," Luther wrote against Latomus, a papist opponent, not a mere *translatio verborum*, "a change in words."[41]

What stands behind Luther's breakthrough interpretation of Paul's "righteousness of God," then, is the biblical depiction of God *who comes*, quite in contrast then, to the depiction of God who *abides above* in eternal self-contemplation. Schooled in Aristotelian scholasticism, the monk Luther had taken for granted that the righteousness in question was a quality of God's divinely perfect being by which God naturally measures creatures for conformity to perfect being. Conformity to God or correspondence to God's natural perfection is further assumed to be the condition for admission to the divine presence, which would be human salvation. This divine standard of righteousness was being taken as the very content of the gospel; Christ gives us the criterion of judgment by which we can measure ourselves if we want to enter into God's eternal presence and so be saved. Not only does this turn the supposedly good news of the gospel into a new version of the same old *monotheism and morality*; as we have seen, though Luther feared damnation, he just did not *want* to enter the presence of the perfect being whom he had come to hate. In this respect, too, Luther foreshadows Nietzsche and today's post-Christendom culture. But unlike Nietzsche and today's culture, Luther broke through to an understanding of the God of the gospel as the *saving Trinity*—the self-surpassing Father who spared not His own Son but gave Him up for us all so that unified with Him by the Spirit, we might be returned to God now and forever.

He had come to hate the perfect being also on account of a corollary "philosophical" assumption, namely, that the human acquisition of righteousness to meet the standard of divine perfection and so merit bliss was, as Luther had learned from teaching Aristotle's ethics, a matter of habitual practice in good works until they became second nature. Just as parents teach children to do otherwise unattractive things like clean their rooms or take out the garbage until the child grows into a proud and joyful performance of duty, so also one becomes good in God's eyes by repeating prayers, abstaining from foods or sexual pleasures, or undertaking pilgrimages or other religious works until the love of God instead of creatures becomes second nature in us. One becomes good by repeatedly doing good until one enjoys doing good.

But not only does this pedagogy separate love for God from love for creatures, it presumes what for Luther is lacking: the good will Aristotle presumed in speaking of parent and child, tutor and pupil. Truth be told, however, even this presumption of Aristotle is rosy. Not a few children have found themselves hating parents and even more pupils exist who have hated their teachers and vice versa. All the more so in relation to heaven. Truly good works presuppose goodwill, but the human will is always already captured to self-seeking. Not only then do religious works not help; they make the bondage worse because of a self-deception involved, as if such forced works are truly good. This self-deception is true both subjectively and objectively. Objectively, religious works cannot consist in the merely quotidian matters of ordinary life in the world: changing the baby's diapers, sticking with the troubled child, enduring faithfully on the job the trials of envious peers, greedy bosses, and uncaring subordinates. Religious works must be super-meritorious, sacrifices invented to impress, self-chosen spectacles: for Luther, such were celibacy, fasting, and pilgrimage, which *intend* to show a religious separation from the competing love for creatures in an exclusive love for God alone. Yet subjectively, the self who seeks self in avoiding the pain of hell and finding pleasure in the hope of heaven remains intact. Its desire for self—or, as Nietzsche put it, its will-to-power—is only sublimated in religion. It seeks not God, but itself in God. And at the same time it is full of resentment for the sacrifice of creaturely loves required in its religious self-deception but enjoyed by the irreligious. How deep the bondage runs!

THE JOYFUL EXCHANGE

Religious works, for Luther, are not good works. The conversion of Paul on the road to Damascus shows this dramatically. They do not deliver the servile self; they compound the bondage, playing on fears and enticing with promised pleasures until the unexpected word from God concerning His Son breaks in to shatter and transform the self-seeking self to make out of it a new creation. As in Paul, here an exchange takes place; an unexpected divine economy is revealed in it. For Luther the sinner-seeking Son gives Himself for the self-seeking sinner so that the one who would ascend to heaven is undone by the One who comes to earth. This salutary undoing and redoing of the subject, however, is no brutal fiat. It is exchange, circulation of life, economy. But it is a happy, amazingly good, joyful exchange, not tit for tat, quid pro quo.

The "joyful exchange," as Luther named it, is from one perspective a divine thievery of the self-seeking self who wants to earn heaven: the Son demands and takes away the sin of the world, not with a magic wand that disappears it into thin air, but rather the Son takes it upon his own anguished soul and tortured body to bear it to death and bury it forever in the tomb. It is from another perspective a gift without remainder, since it gives precisely what is not deserved, thus outbidding and exploding every calculating economy based upon the *suum cuique*, not "giving to each its own," but instead giving innocence for guilt, life for death, righteousness for unrighteousness. And from yet another angle, it brings about true justice in the truly good works that flow forth from the new self that give God the glory that is His due for all His mercy in Christ by working the justice of love seeking structures of mutuality and reciprocity. The sinner is justified by faith and faith in turn reciprocates, giving glory to God and love to the neighbor and hope for the world. So effective justice is aborning in the unjust world, not from demanding it, but by God's one-sidedly giving it in Christ's joyful exchange.

Luther consistently exposited his doctrine of justification in the dramatically participatory and communal language of the joyful interchange between faith and Christ, the bride and bridegroom. As Jared Wicks explains,

53

At the exact center of spiritual existence, according to Luther, the believer is realizing his situation as one of participation and exchange with Christ, of Christ's inhesion and cementing him to himself, and of a transforming exchange between his sin and Christ's righteousness. In "apprehending faith" I lay hold of his victory as the death of my sin and of his consummate righteousness as mine by grace. In passivity under the rapture of grace, I am taken out of my lost state into the sphere of Christ's invincible righteousness.[42]

Thus this righteousness is Christ himself, the God who undertook as a human being to redeem sinners: "But if it is true faith, it is a sure trust and firm acceptance in the heart. It takes hold of Christ in such a way that Christ is the object of faith, or rather not the object but, so to speak, the One who is present in faith itself (*in ipsa fide Christus adest*)." This means that "faith is not mere historical faith, oriented to the distant past, but nothing else than faith formed by Christ (*fides Christo formata*), wherein the living Christ exercises lordship over the total life of the disciples."[43]

In 1519, Luther was already drawing the ecclesiological implications of this. He writes of Augustine's idea of the whole Christ, the Head with His body:

Christ with all his saints, by his love, takes upon himself our present form [Phil 2:7], fights with us against sin, death and all evil. This enkindles in us such love that we take on his form, rely upon his righteousness, life and blessedness. And through this interchange of his blessings and our misfortunes we become one loaf, one bread, one body, one drink, and have all things in common. O this is a great sacrament![44]

Such had been Luther's breakthrough, as he traced his course in memory now. Where had he somehow gone wrong that such beautiful theology would land him in purgatory with the antichrist?

MEMORY RANSACKED: LEO

L eo, too, had to ransack memory. For Luther's surmise was correct: Leo had been preoccupied with matters of high politics and was not sufficiently cognizant of the gravity of the Luther case.[1] When the bull indicting Luther's heresies was finally ready, Leo had to be tracked down by Eck in a hunting camp to obtain final approval for its release and transmission.[2] Exhausted by the intrigues involved in checking the election of Charles of Spain in favor of Frederick, he got the news of Luther's execution a year later in the same hunting camp, where he often retreated from his cares. He was in any case not inclined carefully to think through the precise challenge Luther had posed theologically to the traffic in indulgences, but decided to condemn Luther's teaching "wholesale without sufficient regard to the distinction of their individual degrees of offensiveness."[3] Needless to say, he was even less inclined to make note of the appeal Luther was making to Leo's pastoral responsibility to correct the German "papists" for abuse of his own office, dependent as he was on the income stream these provided.

The fact, as we have seen, was that opposition to Luther had first arisen, not in the Vatican, but at home in Germany, where the issue he raised about the trafficking of divine pardon had put flame to dry tinder. The argument there for indulgences could be made on its own merits only with great difficulty after Luther's critique had become known. Already Tetzel, the merchant of indulgences whom Luther first criticized, made the switch from the question about Christ at stake in indulgences to papal authority, when he wrote that many "will be led to despise the supremacy and authority of the Pope and the Holy Roman see. Works of sacramental satisfaction will be left undone. Preachers and teachers will no longer be believed. Each person will interpret Holy Scripture just as he pleases...each one will learn to believe just what he chooses."[4] As Ludwig Pastor observes from a traditional Roman Catholic perspective, "Indulgences, as something incidental to the main point at issue, soon disappeared from these polemical discussions; but, on the other hand, the question of the authority of the Church always remained in the foreground."[5] In reality, the question of indulgences touching upon the primacy of the gospel in the life of the church was not "incidental," and in switching to the question of the authority of the church, the "papist" opponents in Germany threw fuel on the fire.

In that Luther had challenged *any* authority to issue indulgences in the sense of remission of guilt and *limited* authority to pardon only to the church's own disciplinary penalties, Luther became guilty in their eyes, so to say, *a priori* and *as such*. Nothing about indulgences could even be discussed until Luther submitted unconditionally to papal authority. As a result, the merit of his theological argument for the Christian life as a journey of lifelong repentance from which an indulgent reprieve from cross-bearing detracted rather than aided counted for nothing in their eyes. His conscientious request that his specific errors in this respect be shown to him from Scripture and evident reason had to be ignored on principle. Nothing could be discussed until Luther acknowledged the right of the pope to define theological issues—never mind the *petitio principi*—beginning with the theological issue of the authority of the pope to define theological issues.

Still, Leo did try at least among loyalists to clarify his own understanding. He held that "by virtue of the power of the keys, the Pope can remit both the guilt and the punishment due to actual sins—the guilt by the sacrament of penance and the temporal punishment by indulgences; and that he can, as occasion arises, draw from the overflowing treasury of the merits of Christ and His saints, and grant remissions to faithful

Christians whether they are in this life or in purgatory, united to Christ by love."[6] He has absolute power to do this for the living and the power of intercessory prayer to do so for the dead, such that "all who obtain these indulgences are freed from the amount of temporal punishment which is in proportion with the indulgence granted and obtained."[7] Alas, his present situation—sentenced indefinitely to confined quarters with the heretic who had denied this power to him—spoke against that theory.

While the gist of Luther's case in the Ninety-Five Theses was eclipsed on the Roman side by the assertion of the first principle, so to speak, of papal authority, this confusion was compounded by the counterassertion from Luther's side of the doctrine of justification by faith as an alternative first principle, the so-called article of faith on which the church stands and falls. All the fears beginning with Tetzel that Luther reduced author-ity in the church to individual conscience seemed thus all the more to be reinforced. The issue between the two parties in this way transposed to one of authority in the church, whether of the pope or of the doctrine of justification. This reframing of the issues under dispute represents a devel-opment beyond the origin of the controversy in Luther's attack on the sale of indulgences on behalf of the true treasure of the church, the gospel of the grace and glory of God.

Even if, as we have heard, the sale of indulgences for the dead were possible, Luther had asked in the Ninety-Five Theses, why would a true Christian seeking holiness there want such help? His contemporaneously developed "theology of the cross," to the contrary, *welcomed* "penalties and the cross" as the *divine* work for the soul's *purification* from sin. Luther's at first *limited* critique of papal authority came about as a by-product of this argument, since Luther appealed in the Ninety-Five Theses to the pope's own authority to correct the "papists" for discrediting his pastoral office by overstating their claims in his name. Only in 1520, after Luther had stud-ied Valla's exposé of the medieval forgery of *The Donation of Constantine*, alleging that the first Christian emperor had bequeathed temporal rule also to the Roman bishop, did Luther move toward the categorical judg-ment against the papal institution as antichrist. While he denied that the primacy of the Roman see and its bishop was given by divine right, that is, by direct institution of Christ, he conceded at least in the Latin West the "human right of the pope" that is, as indirectly developed in history under the ostensive guidance of the Spirit. To this point, he "did not draw the conclusion, namely, that the pope must be of the devil."[8] Precisely. In the Ninety-Five Theses the argument was that the office of the keys (figured symbolically on the papal flag unfurled over the indulgence sellers) was not in the sole possession of Peter and his successors, but belonged to the entire Christian community—even if Peter, his successors, or others administered the keys on behalf of the community. The true treasury of the church, in any case, is not the surplus merit of the saints that could be bartered, but the gospel of the grace and glory of God supplying the infinite merit of Christ gratis.

In the interim confusion about what was really at issue, much delay came about in Rome's handling of the Luther case. Even though Leo had summoned Luther to Rome for a hearing early on, the Elector Frederick had insisted that Luther be tried in a German court. So intense was the resentment and distrust of Rome in his region that only a German verdict, he reasoned, could quell popular support of Luther. So it was only after several false starts stretching from the fall of 1517 to the summer of 1521 that the German Dominican, Johannes Eck, finally took matters in hand.[9] He was the one who had first succeeded in extracting an explicit challenge to papal authority from Luther in a 1519 debate in Leipzig. Consequently he had traveled to Rome to pursue indictment of Luther's heresies and finally gained authority over the juridical process. Luther's considered judgment on Eck's character pronounced him an opportunist. Having gotten Luther to deny the papacy's authority by "divine right," "a wide field was open to him and a supreme occasion to flatter in praiseworthy manner the pope and merit his favor, also to ruin me with hate and envy."[10] To the extent that this is right, however, Leo came to rely overly on an interested party from Germany, itself a partisan in the controversy, dependent as Leo was on the funding supplied to him through the sale of indulgences in his name.

Like an indulgent parent who spares the rod, "indulgences" were conceived of by Leo and his court as remissions from deserved punishment.

An important distinction was thus involved between the *guilt* of sin, which violated the baptismal state of grace, on the one hand, and its *punishment*, on the other, which supposedly compensated for the damage to self and others done by sin, and thus it restored moral order to God's world and honor to God's reputation. Only God for His mercy's sake could and did forgive the guilt of sin through the sacrament of penance. This gift of God restored the broken baptismal relationship with the penitent to a state of grace. Indulgences accordingly could only validly be offered to those who sins were forgiven by God and thus in a state of grace.

If that is the case, indulgences *do* help in just the way that presidential pardons or commutations of sentences help the imprisoned. The forgiven, like the thief on the cross who died alongside Jesus, still faced just punishment for his sins. Alongside of the mercy of forgiveness of guilt, justice had still to be satisfied and moral order restored. God mercifully forgives the sinner but justly still hates the sin, and this divine wrath has to be expiated by punishment. Thus it was a misconception, strictly speaking, that Luther popularized, if one asserts that indulgences bought and sold the forgiveness of sins and the remission of guilt rather than the remission of punishment—even if, as Pastor concedes, Tetzel's doctrine was virtually that of the drastic proverb: "As soon as money in the coffer rings, the soul from purgatory's fire springs."[11] The misconception that Luther further popularized in a hostile way was already, then, that of Tetzel and, no doubt, the common people who bought his wares. Indulgences, however, did "buy" something; as almsgiving "buys" relief for the poor, indulgences bought pardon or amnesty or commutation of a sentence for those being punished. Taking payment as a sign of sincerity, then, the purchase of an indulgence brought about merciful reduction in the satisfaction the sinner owed to divine justice and would otherwise pay for in purgatorial sufferings. The presupposition, not wholly dissimilar to Luther's theology of the cross, was that punishment satisfied divine honor, justifying God in His just judgment on sin, though the danger, also in Luther's theology of the cross, was that one could regard the suffering of punishment as meritorious, as if the more one hated oneself the more God loved.

So far as these notions had gained currency, then, the further thought evolved that, following the example of the Lord Jesus, one could in Christian love substitute the merit one has acquired for the lack of merit in one in need of satisfying the required punishment, as especially might be the case of the living for the sake of the dead. This resource was the treasury of surplus merit and was at the disposal of the pope as head of the church who possessed the office of the keys that Jesus had bequeathed to Peter. He had at his disposal a treasure chest of surplus merit from Christ, Mary, and the saints, which could be applied to the account of others. The purchase of an indulgence for the helpless dead suffering in purgatory, hence, was a good work of love. One sacrificed hard-earned money out of love to relieve those suffering for their sins in purgatory in the hope that both self and loved one, already forgiven by God, would sooner be received by God in paradise.

As we have heard, Luther's initial challenge to the sale of indulgences in the Ninety-Five Theses was executed within this common frame of reference. He denied neither the need for forgiveness, the necessity of punishment or of a postmortem purgatory, the treasury of merit, nor the authority of the pope. Indeed, the only thing he denied, and his principle concern, was the short-circuiting of the sinner's needed repentance by, as he alleged, the cheap grace of buying pardon rather than bearing one's cross already now, indeed so long as it takes to be delivered from sinful desire to holy desire. But Luther's nuance was lost on Leo.

The complexity of the deal Leo had made for the sale of a new round of indulgences in Germany that provoked Luther's protest betrayed a convoluted intertwining of powers and interests.[12] The episcopacy was still elected by local ecclesiastical authorities, with Rome's approval. In a feudal society, however, this meant that the local nobility controlled ecclesiastical nominations and that the bishops in large remained representatives of the nobility and their interests. Albrecht of Brandenburg became bishop of the region to the north and west of Luther's Saxony, but he wished to have charge of (and thus also income from) more than one diocese. This was forbidden by canon law. Papal permission to hold more than one diocese was as expensive as the extra office itself was lucrative. To pay for the privilege the deal was negotiated that a new papal indulgence would be announced, splitting the income between Albrecht and Leo. Leo's motive in this particular case was financial support for one of his own good works: making the basilica of St. Peter in Rome into a finished and fitting home for the artistic works of the divine Raphael and the incomparable Michelangelo.[13]

Ornament this was, but not mere ornament. Art is never merely decorative. Art *symbolizes* in a sense that Leo had internalized growing up in the wealthy house of the upwardly mobile burgher family, the Medicis of Florence, and under the tutelage of the Neoplatonist Renaissance thinkers. Neoplatonists were those who conceived of the cosmic system as ordered by a dynamic flow in a great chain of being proceeding from God on high downward to lend form and order to matter and thence returning from multiplicity to unity in God in the ascent of the rational soul. The "paganism," if the term can be used here without prejudice, of the scheme was manifest in depictions of the ancient Roman and Greek myths of the gods right alongside depictions of the biblical stories and saints. Indeed, among Leo's influential tutors was the humanist, Marsilio Ficino, who, as Pastor soberly observed, "had made the hazardous attempt to combine the platonic cultus with Christianity."[14] This Neoplatonic symbolization in art of the great chain of being was an alternative, even rival version of the humanist Renaissance that Luther imbibed along the lines of Valla.

But it was a "humanism!" As the microcosm of the great cosmic system, the human being mediated the intercourse between things above and things below, as depicted in Michelangelo's famous rendering of the creation of Adam on the ceiling of the Sistine Chapel. This image was hardly mere decoration. It proclaimed a humanocentric truth about the world, "man the measure of all things"; even God the Father there depicted is in Adam's image writ large. So likewise, as mentioned, the abundant incorporations in Florentine art of motifs and images from Greek and Roman mythology. No longer taken as idolatrous threats to exclusive biblical monotheism, but as representations of the splendid ranks of the cosmic order, the gods of ancient Rome and Greece, too, were absorbed in the grand synthesis of Renaissance art under the auspices of Neoplatonism.

Leo became the great patron of this vision of reality, and no one in his circle, as Pastor wrote, "was scandalized by this mixture of Christianity and paganism."[15] On the contrary, the artistic "despoiling" of the treasures of the pagans represented the maturation of Christendom to them. Like humanists who followed in Valla's train, these humanists, too—let us call them the "Neoplatonists" in distinctions from Valla's *literati*—were done with the medieval theology of the schools. In the pretension to scientific method, scholastic theology had become futile, as it seemed to them, in the pursuit of increasingly remote and academic partisanships.[16] The Neoplatonists, too, were seeking a new way forward for inquiry that would meet the emerging cultural situation, which challenged humanity to rise up maturely to its divine vocation as measure of all things. The need was urgent. The old ways of scholasticism could neither meet the massive changes now occurring nor would they survive them.

It was an age of anxiety, religiously speaking. The world-wide trade flowing through mercantile Venice, financed by the rise of big banking to back such entrepreneurial adventures, coupled with urbanization throughout Europe and the rise of the university, brought home the discovery of new, exotic cultural and indeed geographical worlds both East and West. The world was a much bigger place than previously imagined. The need for government bureaucrats educated in languages and able to read foreign texts well to negotiate deals, enforce contracts and exact taxation attended the corresponding rise in Europe of early nation-states, which in turn required stronger central governments, as Florence's Machiavelli described in his prescient work *The Prince*.

All this cultural change combined to produce a definite, worldly-wise skepticism regarding the religious certitudes inherited from the preceding eight centuries of Christendom. Europe had first attained self-consciousness and a sense of unity as a new, that is, *holy* Roman Empire poised alike against Byzantium and Islam, when the pope crowned Charlemagne, whose grandfather, Charles "The Hammer" Martel, had stopped the Arab Muslim advance from Spain through the Pyrenees.[17] The symbiosis of emperor and pope henceforth characterized the rise of Europe in the centuries between the Dark Ages following the fall of the Western Roman Empire and the Renaissance into which Leo was born.

But the economic, social, and political changes that had now brought a burgher family like the Medicis to power in Florence just so worked curiosity about possibilities other than the customary arrangements of Christendom. Since the Dark Ages, the customary arrangement had been the symbiosis of Christianization with feudalism. Warlords became aristocracy, who invited the monastery to safety within castle walls. In exchange, the monks evangelized and educated the peasants. But this arrangement effectively created a vast multitude of fiefdoms as often as not warring with each other.[18] The needed modernization by the time of the Renaissance was to secure the political autonomy of the papacy so that it could unify Europe both culturally and politically against Islam, recently turned back in Spain to Africa in one form, but now knocking at the rear door of Europe in another form, the Ottoman Turks besieging Vienna.

Raphael's *Coronation of Charlemagne*. From 1519, when Leo hoped to ally with Francis I as the new Holy Roman Emperor. Raphael painted Francis's face on Charlemagne and Leo's on Pope Leo III's.

Leo's papacy was thus intended to modernize the institution to master this new set of circumstances, just as his father, Lorenzo the Magnificent, had modernized Florence. Just this strategy, however, contained a certain blind spot that eventually sabotaged the effort. The "prince" no longer needed to have "noble" blood coursing through his veins just because the liquid power of money was overtaking the feudal order based on possession of land. This rise of capital is what Leo did not and could not see, even though the worldliness of Rome in this regard had become notorious. Indeed, Leo's own father, Lorenzo, had warned his son when he first went to live in Rome that it was a "sink of iniquity."[19] At the end of the Fifth Lateran Council in 1516 the esteemed humanist Pico della Mirandola[20] delivered in Leo's presence a caustic speech urgently calling for the reform of morals in a church that had become the object of satire and derision for its hypocrisies among the humanist "poets." Chief among Rome's moral offenses was simony, the buying and selling of church offices. The corruption was obvious for all—including Leo—to see. But Leo himself had become a cardinal at the age of seven in just this way of simony by his father's donations to the church, and Leo was himself adept in such wheeling and dealing.

Thus calls for moral reform of Rome's pretensions to courtly prestige[21] financed by simony, indulgences, and deficit spending fell on Leo's deaf ears. Much more immediate in his eyes were tumultuous geopolitical events: the collapse of Christian rival Byzantium before the hostile Ottoman Turk advance under the banner of Islam and the nigh unto interminable warfare between Christian nations in Europe. Internal conflict made for paralysis before the external aggression that threatened to actualize a real but very unattractive possibility for governing Europe other than traditional Christendom. Leo's response to the calls for reform, therefore, was to focus on consolidating the papacy as a politically independent spiritual leader of Western Christianity under the geopolitical banner of the "freedom of Italy."[22]

Secured geopolitically, then, the papacy would be in a position by virtue, its cultural power in the Petrine office of the keys—negatively the ban or excommunication and positively the sale of indulgences—to stop the warfare among Christians and unite them in a crusade against Islam. So keen on this crusade was Leo that for a time he was willing personally to lead it (he had spent years of his apprenticeship under the warrior pope Julian as chaplain to troops on the front lines).[23] But this strategic decision meant that he turned a blind eye to the internal decay of morals that Pico identified and could not cognize the theological diagnosis of its root in Luther.[24] While report of Leo's extravagance at court and in pageantry has often been seen as a moral weakness of profligacy in Leo and thus the cause of his failing to grasp the gravity of the Luther affair,[25] the extravagance, which did indeed keep Leo perpetually one step ahead of the debt collectors, had more to do, according to the conventions of the day, with cultivation of the Vatican as an independent political force.[26] Leo thought of his Curia as a revival of ancient Rome and indeed his salon there was "the Paris of its day."[27]

Personally, he had been alienated from the severity of Augustinianism from childhood by the experience in Florence of the ascetic moralism and fire-and-brimstone preaching of Savonrola's gloomy demand for austerity in a new age brimming with human possibilities. A child of affluence, he was fond of gaiety and banter, life and laughter, pomp and circumstance, and his favorite aristocratic pastime, the chase. Pageantry,[28] extravagance (and corresponding debt),[29] courtly glory,[30] and patronage of the arts[31] in pursuit of the papacy's cultural prestige would combine to symbolize the centering of the cosmic harmony in Rome, uniting Christians against Islam and supplanting rival Christian Byzantium in the process. This was Leo's way forward amid the challenges of the day. But to those outside Rome's orbit the symbolism seemed increasingly hollow.

Leo's life, not without its own Christian drama, followed the narrow path as he saw it between giving in to the revival of "pagan" resources being rediscovered in the Renaissance and giving up before the advance of Islam. In his Neoplatonic world, personal destiny was a matter of fate, or, in Christian terms, providence. One is not free to do just anything, but rather free to rise up to one's destiny or to flee it and so miss one's destiny. In the first path lies salvation and in the second, ruin.

Leo had notoriously remarked to his brother Guiliano, "Since God has seen fit to give us the papacy, let us enjoy it!"[32] But this was not a cynical remark. It was an affirmation of destiny, *amor fati* ("love of one's fate"). From his father's decision to give his brightest child to an ecclesiastical career already at the age of seven (when, as mentioned, Leo was tonsured and made a cardinal),[33] everything in life had prepared him for, and led him to, the papal coronation in 1513. His dramatic journey to the church's highest office persuaded Leo that the hand of divine blessing rested upon him. Leo "declared cheerfully that men of mark like himself were specially provided for by Heaven, so that they need never lack long for what was necessary, if only they kept a lively faith in their predestined good fortune."[34] Leo walked this talk. This was his Christian faith through times of adversity as well as times of prosperity. It was also, he reflected, confirmed in his own religious experience.

During a revolution, the Medicis had been driven out of Florence when Leo's brother, Piero, did not prove to be the leader their father had been. In the tumult, Leo, too, had to flee while disguised as a poor monk since he had a price of one thousand ducats on his head.[35] But this exile from Florence after the revolution gave the young man Leo opportunity to travel and see the world north of the Alps.[36] As a cardinal, Leo returned to live in Rome upon the ascension of Julius II, whom he served in various capacities, eventually as his secretary of state. His house in Rome, in this interim, became a combination salon and art gallery as he made himself patron of the arts.

The fateful events surrounding the Battle at Ravenna transpired in 1512,[37] which Leo attended as chaplain to the papal army, allied with the Swiss, trying to drive the French out of the north to secure the liberty of Italy. The extremely nearsighted cardinal, mounted on horseback, rode up and down the ranks while rallying the troops. But a catastrophic defeat left twenty thousand troops dying on the field of battle. Leo escaped the battlefield but eventually was betrayed into the hands of the French who found him hiding in the most undignified quarters of a pigeon coop. As in his earlier exile from Florence, fortunes had sunk as low as Leo could have imagined. Yet Leo kept faith and, with the collusion of certain of his captors, escaped once again in disguise, making his way back to Florence to greet the restoration of the rule of the Medicis. From the depths to the heights in a matter of months! As if on cue, Julius II died. And Leo, within a year of the disastrous battle of Ravenna, was elected pope. What a reversal of fortune! "Miraculous," it was deemed, "in an age which attributed all good or evil to the direct intervention of a watchful Providence."[38] Understandably, Leo felt himself confirmed in his faith and in his particular vision of the way forward for a united Christian Europe.

Leo punctuated the miracle of divine Providence with an exclamation point by scheduling his papal coronation on the first-year anniversary of the Battle of Ravenna.[39] He was elected by the college of cardinals for his reputation as a man preferring peace to war—the opposite of Julius II[40]—and for his personal morals,[41] which Luther also acknowledged in various writing prior to his excommunication. Indeed, Leo's first year in office brought widespread acclamation for the "cessation of open warfare" among the nations of Christian Europe, albeit at the price of "an increase of diplomatic intrigue." Leo's profile as public peacemaker exhorting the sovereigns of Europe to "acts of Christian charity and forgiveness,"[42] however, unraveled in the following years. Above all a costly war of revenge against a disloyal fief—the Duke of Urbino—undermined his determination to lead in a way other than the militaristic Julius II. Duplicity in the politics of playing France and Spain and Germany against one another besmirched his moral reputation. A reputation for neglect of office, courtly extravagance, and even buffoonery[43] attended his final days. His death on the hunt in the tusks of a wild boar seemed to confirm all these sad judgments on a papacy that had begun with such promise.

With time on his hands, Leo reflected on the turn of events that had at last brought him to the purgatory of sharing room indefinitely with the heretic whom he had handed over to the flames.

A CONSENSUS ON JUSTIFICATION

L uther was wrong about the gloomy end of the world. Leo was wrong about a rosy future for Christendom. These mutually reinforcing errors brought them together in purgatory until they would converge in a new understanding. The world that God is creating is much greater than Luther could or did imagine, and the future of Christianity in that larger world is not the past of Christendom in which Leo gloried. These erroneous judgments, however, were judgments of a kind that every thinking Christian must make. The reason for this need is that this kind of judgment about God's governance of the world goes back to a perplexity from the very origins of the gospel mission to the nations. The earliest Christians believed in the imminence of the kingdom of God, the nearness of the Parousia of Christ. But where was the day of His coming? The fading of near-expectation is traceable already in the later New Testament writings. But it left the mission to the nations, which it had first inspired, in something of a quandary.

On the one hand, should the mission proceed on the basis of the assumption that the delay of the Parousia was only a postponement, not a falsification of the literal picture of the world's end that one can find, for instance, in Mark 13 or 1 Thessalonians 4 or the Apocalypse of John the Seer? On the other hand, could a deliteralization of the apocalyptic end-time scenario avoid transposing the great expectation of the reign of God into the reality of the church on earth as the visible repository of divine glory? If Luther fell on the former horn of the dilemma, Leo had fallen on the latter. But both erred. In their erroneous judgments, nonetheless, there were elements of truth. Luther was right that his apostle distinguished between the *already* and the *not yet*: *already* Judgment Day breaks into the present in justification by faith, but faith is *not yet* sight and salvation in the sense of the victory over death both individual and cosmic—this victory remains outstanding. Leo was right that the present reality of future salvation was the pilgrim people of God, a social phenomenon greater than individual conversions, which represented and manifested the reign of God.

It is true that what Jesus promised was the kingdom of God, but what we got was the church. But this truth does not entail either Luther's pessimism or Leo's optimism. If, theologically, we proceed with deliteralization (*not* demythologization, that is, denarrativization!), the coming of God is not literally the end of time, but the time of the end, the *kairos* of salvation, which literally happens where and when it pleases God through the announcement of it in the cross and resurrection of Christ. For this time of the end is proclaimed to, and eventuated in, the nations, lived out in the vocation of Christians within them, and manifested by the here-and-now church though it is visible only to the eyes of faith. The church is both the creature of this proclamation and in turn its indispensable instrument in the economy by which God redeems a world fallen prey to idols and demons. The church is not God's kingdom in its fulfillment, the beloved community, but it is its present creature and agent in the world. Neither pessimism nor optimism is permitted by this necessary deliteralization of the apocalyptic picture of a fraught and contested world, but rather attentiveness to the signs of the times is called for. Christian hope negotiates many ends of the world, always hoping against hope for the restoration of the world to a system of blessing and its deliverance from the accursed cycle of violence and counterviolence.

On the way to this new judgment regarding God's relation to human history, however, there were a host of issues for the purgatorial bunk

70

mates to work through. From Luther's side it was chiefly the doctrine of justification by faith alone. From Leo's side it was chiefly the promise of the Holy Spirit to preserve the church from fatal error in teaching the faith; the faith that has objective content and subjectively is never alone but is always accompanied by love and hope, if it is true faith. From this basic standoff a host of subsidiary questions arose surrounding the right understanding and observance of the sacraments, chiefly the implications of the mutual recognition of baptism for church fellowship and the right discernment of the Lord's body in the Eucharistic meal. Lesser matters doctrinally—but of great significance in the devotional life of the church—concerned prayers for the dead, devotion to saints, and veneration of the Virgin Mary.

The long silence after the ransacking of memories was broken when Leo ventured, "Blessed griefwork—isn't that what you said? What is blessed about grief which is irrevocable loss and sorrow and mourning and tears? I understand that this fate is our grief. It is just punishment for our sins. Surely it is that for me and I can imagine that it is also so for you. But how can you think it to be *blessed*?"

"Blessed are those who mourn," Luther replied, ever quick with Scripture on his lips, "for they shall be comforted!"

"The words of our Lord," Leo acknowledged. "I take them on authority, but I do not see how they can be true or apply to us now. I lived for a cause. I *was* that cause—in the flesh, incarnate. And that cause is now taken away from me. Now what remains of me, broken shell of man that I am? With the loss of that cause I was lost as well. What is left of me without my cause? Is there even an 'I' which remains now to mourn?"

"A rhetorical question," Luther snorted. "It is evident to me, though I am tempted to close my eyes at it, that you along with your cause somehow remain right before my eyes. *That* is what *I* cannot understand."

"True, enough. I remain also right before my own eyes. But *my* cause has shipwrecked—on *your* rock. My cause was the unity of Christians, the end of war between them to forge a common stand against the infidel, leading to the victory of the church in history and on earth as the very fulfillment of God's promises. Your reckless preaching that faith alone justifies unraveled all of this, just as John Tetzel warned from the beginning. It undid centuries of civilization-building. It divided Christians who will never agree on anything if each believer gets to decide what the faith is. Not only war but religious war will result among Christians consequently, when the holy crusade should be waged against heretics and aliens like the Muslims. Rather than rising above politics as divine leader, the divided church will become the instrument of each nation or political faction that predominates until it becomes an empty shell."

Luther took Leo's rant without flying into a rage, as had been his earthly custom.

"You know," Luther finally admitted, "this 'unraveling' was always my nightmare. I dreaded the thought that I had somehow wrecked what generations had patiently built. Growing up out of peasant stock on the edge of civilization, I appreciated the covenant of the generations. I knew in my bones the pagan darkness and cultural backwardness from which we had arisen. So I feared when I saw some of my own supposed followers whip up an angry mob to smash the images and statues that adorned St. Mary's church where I preached. I feared this when a former colleague on the faculty gave up his teaching post and tried to live as a common peasant. It was a ludicrous sight. Then a former student, whom I actually helped to acquire his first pastoral post, turned into a wide-eyed revolutionary agitator. By questioning authority, I *did* fear that I had let loose hordes of devils, filling the land, eager to devour us. Already in life, I experience this *shipwreck* of *my* cause. And in bouts of deep depression I questioned all my questioning."

"You feared this? My impression was that you intended this! What else could faith alone imply?"

"Hope and love, I thought, just as you said a moment ago."

"If faith is alone," Leo pressed, "how can it imply *anything* else, let alone love and hope?"

Luther clarified. "You must discern the antithesis, not fly off into inferences not intended. You discern the antithesis of the affirmation of faith alone when you attend to the context of the claim to see what precisely is being excluded. Love and hope are not being excluded. Faith, too, works;

72

in fact it is operative in love. That is not the antithesis precisely stated. The claim is that in the matter of our justification before God faith suffices apart from performance of the works of the law. Don't you see that faith, too, would be excluded if we take faith as a work of the law, that is, if faith means something I perform, like *my* choice for Jesus, *my* decision to be a Christian, *my* will to believe? But the Lord says, 'You did not choose me. I chose you.' Faith alone is faith that says in response to this word of the Lord, 'Amen! Let it be for me as the Lord has spoken.'"

"For the 'work of the law,'" Luther continued, "is whatever *I* do as child of Adam so far as it is under constraint, then, whether of promise of reward or threat of punishment. It is a servile obedience, avoiding pain and seeking pleasure, intended to secure my self-seeking self. But justifying faith is something new. It is a new subjectivity, a new birth given from above. Faith is something that Christ did for me and now effects in me by the gift of His Spirit. Faith is what Jesus performed for us who are otherwise incapable of such faith. That is why the addition of the little particle, alone, is so necessary. Otherwise, as Plato taught us, we take 'faith' as a human work and indeed as a pathetic work, the lowest form of knowledge that accepts things on the basis of authority. But Paul is not Plato! If you are thinking in this philosophical way, then of course you will think that faith alone is dead knowledge of a fact that must be livened with works of love and hope. But the premise is wrong. Faith is not the human work of believing this or that. Faith is the Spirit's own 'Yes' and 'Amen' in me to the word of Christ spoken for me and to me. So it is not my human faith in a reported fact plus my more important human works of the law that justify, but faith alone in Christ alone by the grace of the faith-imparting Spirit alone that makes us right with the God who sends His Son and Spirit so to wrest us from the jaws of hell and bring us to His kingdom."

"Faith without works is dead," Leo retorted, grinning that he could quote back Scripture as well.

"Of course it is dead without works," Luther agreed. "As I said and have said repeatedly, faith alone is operative in love and hope; the same Apostle Paul says both these things without any hint of contradiction. What is lacking in your grasp of Paul's meaning is that faith is not just any

73

human opinion but faith in Jesus as the Christ, that is, as the saving righteousness supplied for us by God to count before God. No one receives that on the basis of mere authority. It is not visible fact that human eyes simply see. No one understands the gospel claim to truth in the power of natural reason. Here is a quid without a pro quo, a gift without strings, a joyful, not a commercial exchange of our evil for His good. Who can credit that? Faith alone lives—*only*!—because *Jesus lives*. If Christ is not risen, our faith is in vain and we are still dead in our sins. You cannot understand faith alone unless you also understand its correlate or object, Christ alone the crucified and risen redeemer of the world."

Leo nodded. "This is much clearer. It is much clearer when you talk about Christ and His divine work for us and for all.[1] We know that *the Father sent his Son into the world to save sinners. The foundation and presupposition of justification is the incarnation, death, and resurrection of Christ. Justification thus means that Christ himself is our righteousness, in which we share through the Holy Spirit in accord with the will of the Father.*[2] This affirmation about Christ and His meaning for us is much clearer to me than saying abstractly that we are justified by faith alone. It becomes muddy in my eyes when you put the focus on the believer rather than on Him who is believed. For anyone who looks on Christ sees that He was justified both by his faith and his work of obedience, even to death on a cross. Must we not follow in His train?"

"We *get to* follow in His train," Luther softly said, correcting Leo's implication. "The apostle contrasts the obedience of the slave to the obedience of children, obedience to the law, and the obedience of faith. We *get* to follow Jesus, as newborn children of God want and will and desire with all their hearts, that is, if faith is true and not phony. *Together we should confess: By grace alone, in faith in Christ's saving work and not because of any merit on our part, we are accepted by God and receive the Holy Spirit, who renews our hearts while equipping and calling us to good works.* Good fruit comes forth from this root. *When the justified live in Christ and act in the grace they receive, they bring forth, in biblical terms, good fruit. Since Christians struggle against sin their entire lives, this consequence of justification is also for them an obligation they must fulfill.* Thus both Jesus and the apostolic

74

Scriptures admonish Christians to bring forth the works of love. There is an indicative of grace: You are children of God! And on this basis an imperative of grace: Live as children of God! If the heart sets all its fear, trust, and love in the God of grace, faith is a living, mighty thing that cannot be idle but springs into action for others as Christ sprang into action for us one and all. If one does not spring into action for others in love, then one is obligated afresh to examine the heart and test one's faith. But if we as theologians are to make this priority and sufficiency of grace unmistakably clear, we must exclude the ideas that either our feeling of renewal or subsequent works of love are meritorious with respect to God's gracious justification. Our renewal to faith is prior and it is gift of the Spirit. It is God's gracious justification in the very fact that it evokes the new subjectivity of faith."

"This seems extreme to me," Leo observed. "Does not this sharp exclusion of the natural man with his natural self-love exclude real human beings, persons who cannot help but be interested in their own lives, fates, destinies, whether they please God and go to heaven or displease God and fail to attain the great goal of life eternal? In talking this way, do you not risk turning human beings into automatons deprived of consent and cooperation in their own salvation? No one denies that it is all by grace. By God's grace we are created and destined to salvation. By God's grace we are awakened from our sloth to be concerned for our salvation; by grace we find the fountain of grace in the sacraments of the church that are generously provided for us there. By grace we apply ourselves to grace. And by grace God crowns His own gifts when He rewards our little but real merit, which is our own personal consent and active cooperation with His grace." Leo was pleased that with that last thought he could throw a little bit of Augustine back into Luther's face.

"Listen to you!" Luther howled, returning to his earthly style. "You turn grace into such a general principle that it loses its Christ-focus, particularly as the good pleasure or favor of God poured out on us sinners when were still weak and indeed enemies. You dilute grace into an idea of God's graciousness and think that we have it when all we do is think this way. What is this but to bypass the cross? The cross of Christ who died for us as sinners? The cross of Christ laid upon us sinners so that we die with Him!?"

"Of course that would be true, but you miss my meaning," Leo insisted in the face of Luther's rant. "What Christian does not know that freedom *in relation to persons and the things of this world is no freedom in relation to salvation, for as sinners they stand under God's judgment and are incapable of turning by themselves to God to seek deliverance, of meriting their justification before God, or of attaining salvation by their own abilities?* I see this and I have seen God's hand in guiding my path in life. Even now especially I see it that in spite of the ruin I have made and the shipwreck of my cause, I stand as a sinner under God's judgment. Yet how am 'I' to be forgiven and cleansed, if no 'I' remains under this piercing scrutiny of God? Is it not now 'I' who perceives and receives this, letting myself be turned anew to God?"

Luther uncharacteristically remained silent and let Leo continue.

"So perhaps I do now see how the notion of 'merit' can mislead you to think that I imagine natural human powers capable of self-salvation. But my dear man, I am a student of Augustine and St. Thomas, not of Scotus, Occam, or Biel, those modern theologians whom you read instead.[3] Moreover, isn't the Bible, including the New Testament, including the Beatitude that you quoted to me earlier—'Blessed are they that mourn, for they shall be comforted'—isn't such talk of our 'reward' everywhere present in Scripture, saturating it really? Doesn't faith itself look forward in hope to the fulfillment of God's promise? Listen to me and hear what I truly affirm when I say that we *'cooperate' in preparing for and accepting justification by consenting to God's justifying action:* I mean *such personal consent as itself an effect of grace, not as an action arising from innate human abilities.* Isn't that exactly the same thing that you describe as faith that justifies, faith that personally appropriates the gift of God and affirms that it apply also 'for me'? Help me here, for I see no alternative to this explanation of faith as personal consent, as blessed Mary's 'Let it be unto me as the Lord says.' Otherwise you force us into the awful teaching of double predestination, reducing human persons arbitrarily to objects of benevolence or wrath so that there would be no human difference between persons damned or saved but only the arbitrary choice of a divine bully."

"There is no difference between persons damned or saved," Luther snapped back, "if we look to them as persons apart from the favor of God poured out on sinners in Christ. Moreover, this pouring out of divine love on sinners is what makes the damned to be saved. And they are saved because faith is evoked by the extraordinary love for sinners shed abroad in their hearts by the inner testimony of the Holy Spirit corresponding to the outer testimony of the gospel word. The work of gifting faith to receive the gift, which is Christ as our righteousness, is the sovereign work of the Spirit who blows as He will. We are at the mercy of the Spirit!"

Leo kept his peace. He knew now that they were both at the mercy of the Spirit.

So Luther continued: "But don't ask me about double predestination. I flee from the thought in horror because it is what reason infers by the light of nature. But faith reasons otherwise by the light of the grace of God known in Christ that God is and will be seen to be just, not arbitrary, in the light of glory. Consequently I look solely to the revealed God in Christ and do not speculate about a hidden God apart from Christ. So when I *exclude any possibility of contributing to one's own justification, I do not deny that believers are fully involved personally in their faith, which is effected by God's Word.*"

"Very good," Leo agreed. "It seems, then, that we are not so far apart. But still I ask you. Is the world so big and God so small that only those who are effectively called in this life can be saved? Has God created the many to pluck but those few who believe like a Luther from the fire? That sounds more like the heresy of the gnostic elitists of old than the universal grace of God everywhere believed by all in the church, which is genuinely catholic. Surely we should say together that *all people are called by God to salvation in Christ* and we should affirm together that this divine calling is not a mere wish, but the effective will of the almighty God. But if so, who is it now who limits the scope of God's grace only to those who come to faith in this life? Does not your own Paul conclude his long meditation on predestination to salvation in the Letter to the Romans with the mystery that God has consigned all to sin in order to have mercy on all?"

"The words of Paul I cannot deny. But neither can I comprehend yet what they mean," Luther said quietly, recognizing the conundrum. Deny freedom, and you seem implicated in a doctrine of double predestination, if faith justifies but only some are granted faith. Affirm freedom, and you allow human merit to segregate the sheep from the goats. "I cannot yet comprehend yet what Paul's words of universal salvation mean because I am still here with you in purgatory; we have not yet entered into the light of glory to see how God is just in God's choices. We only see so far as the light of grace allows. Here what we see plainly is that *God forgives sin by grace and at the same time frees human beings from sin's enslaving power and imparts the gift of new life in Christ. When persons come by faith to share in Christ, God no longer imputes to them their sin and through the Holy Spirit effects in them an active love. These two aspects of God's gracious action are not to be separated, for persons are by faith united with Christ, who in his person is our righteousness.*"

In this move—or dodge—Luther turned the conversation away from speculation back to what may be seen here and now in the light of grace. What may be seen by faith in the light of grace is that faith is a union with Christ. As Paul once wrote, "It is no longer I who live but Christ who lives in me." That is a statement that, as Leo feared, seems to annihilate the human person. But Paul immediately added, "And the life I now live in the flesh, I live by faith in (or the faithfulness of) the Son of God who loved me and gave Himself for me." This is a statement that admits the continuing existence of the "I." The reconciliation of these two side-by-side affirmations is that Christ is present in faith, and faith is a personal union with the present Christ. Faith believes both God's love for us who are against God and God's love in us who have come to be for God. These aspects of divine love for human beings are inseparable because Christ died for those who are against God and Christ rose to bring those for whom He died to belong to the cause of God.

"If these two aspects are not to be separated," Leo was thinking out loud, "then *God's forgiving grace always brings with it a gift of new life,*

78

which in the Holy Spirit becomes effective in active love. That is clear enough. It satisfies my concern that by faith alone you excluded newness of life and the redemption and sanctification of the created 'I.'"

"Yes," Luther interrupted, "I do believe that God created me with all that exists and that Christ has redeemed me, a lost and condemned creature, and that the Holy Spirit has called me through the gospel to faith and the fellowship of the saints."

"Agreed, then," Leo responded. "But it seems to me that you are wrong to deny that *justification is dependent on the life-renewing effects of grace in human beings.* Have you not argued that faith is free, personal, and voluntary and as such a work and gracious gift of the Holy Spirit? Granted that faith in Christ is not a human work. Still, you yourself have repeated specified faith as personal appropriation, 'for me.' Haven't you thus made justification dependent on faith and described faith as human regeneration, the new birth from above as our Lord speaks to Nicodemus in John 3? Assuming now that we have clarified these terms, how can you now retreat from your own doctrine of justification by faith to justification by grace and in the process libel us as teaching justification by works?"

"Agh!" Luther groaned, "I am caught in my own net!"[4] Indeed, he was. In the course of the controversy, followers of Luther began to explain justification as the felt experience of new birth at the infusion of divine righteousness and thus began to refer believers to the examination of their religious affections. This was wrong in Luther's eyes on two counts. First, the righteousness of God in Christ consisted in the Incarnate Son's obedience to death and its vindication by His God and Father on Easter morn. It was not that philosophical idea of essential divine righteousness, a quiescent quality of God now being poured into souls like a liquid transforming them. Second, this righteousness of Christ is the believer's by virtue of the joyful exchange and thus, abstractly speaking, by the imputation of an alien righteousness. To fend off a new form of self-seeking self-absorption and to return followers from introspection to "extraspection," so to say (looking on Christ rather than on themselves), Luther indeed began to backtrack from the particularity of faith to the generality of grace. He allowed the rather different model of a juridical pronouncement to supplement (and in time to supplant) the nuptial model of the joyful exchange. To exclude the idea of faith as a meritorious human work or religious experience that can be cultivated by pious practices and thus felt,[5] he likewise supplemented his early emphasis on faith as a "living, mighty thing" to faith as *vita passiva*, a pure passivity, almost a Buddhist *Gelassenheit*. God's grace does it all! Just let it be! But the rhetorical shift to the monergism of grace allowed him also to heighten the polemic against the papists as synergists. Now it was possible to say something quite false: Protestants teach justification by grace while Catholics teach justification by works. Luther was indeed caught in his own net. Purgatory permitted no artful dodges. And he knew it.

"Look, dear Leo," Luther started afresh, "can we not make the following kind of distinction between faith in the abstract and concrete faith, faith incarnate, so to speak? In the concrete life of the regenerate in the world, the believer is always embattled, always in struggle to love in a loveless world, to hope in a world shorn of hope. In the ebb and flow of this fierce battle, the believer can hardly believe that she believes.[6] If faith rests upon a feeling of faith it becomes faith in faith rather than faith in Christ. Soon as a result it will be exhausted from the battle, lie down, and surrender.

"Let me illustrate. One of the most painful moments of my pastoral practice occurred when I visited a jaded old fellow whom I invited to the services of God's house. He told me that he had been born again so many times, yet it never took. He was beyond redemption, he thought. But we must be born anew every new day from baptism day until resurrection day! He thought this despairing thought, you see, because he was looking at himself for certainty rather than at Christ the friend of sinners who loved him and gave Himself for him. Learning 'extraspection,' or learning to look at Christ and thus to see oneself in Christ while one remains wholly engaged in the world and learning 'to be in the world but not of the world'—who can do this in their own power? Our concrete faith is always ambiguous. It cannot of itself provide the certainty of God's favor in which the 'I' can rest while the same 'I' engages and works. It is the proclaimed Christ who provides the certainty of faith in its daily struggle

against this world, the devil, and the old sinful self. *In the midst of temptation, believers should not look to themselves but look solely to Christ and trust
only him. In trust in God's promise they are assured of their salvation, but are
never secure looking at themselves.*

"So yes, 'faith alone' is an abstraction from the situation of this concrete and embattled believer; but it is a useful and clarifying one that is
the source of consolation and strengthening for the one whose renewal
in love and hope is constantly under stress and strain. Before God, if not
before the world or even before my own self, however, I am 'by faith alone'
God's beloved child solely on account of Christ who has made me His
own, hence by 'grace alone.' Thus *a distinction but not a separation is made
between justification itself and the renewal of one's way of life that necessarily
follows from justification and without which faith does not exist.*"

"Alright, alright," Leo excitedly said. "You admit that justification by
faith alone is an abstraction from the concrete life of Christians in the
world! Excellent! What else is a distinction that is not a separation but
an abstraction? What matters to me is that you here clearly affirm that
concretely *justification and renewal are joined in Christ, who is present in
faith.* So the concrete life of the believer, embattled as you say, consists in
union with Christ, who is present, not absent, and who is at once for us
and also in us!"

"Yes, we are servants of this present Christ, not vicars of an absentee
landlord," Luther noted, thinking ahead in anticipation of a controversy
yet to be discussed.

"The more we converge on Christ, the closer we come to each other,"
Leo again noted. "If it is clear that faith alone is said to justify because of
the Christ in whom the believer personally invests himself, and that this
personal investment is possible because Jesus lives and is and can be present in this saving way to give himself. Catholics can also affirm that *without faith, no justification can take place. Persons are justified through baptism
as hearers of the word and believers in it. This new personal relation to God
is grounded totally on God's graciousness and remains constantly dependent
on the salvific and creative working of this gracious God, who remains true to
himself, so that one can rely upon him.*"

"This indeed is the crucial point," Luther said turning to Leo with special earnestness, "for in justification God puts a stop to all human boasting so that we all learn to glory instead in the cross of the Lord as the costly deed of His love for us one and all. *Thus justifying grace never becomes a human possession to which one could appeal over against God. While Catholic teaching emphasizes the renewal of life by justifying grace, this renewal in faith, hope, and love is always dependent on God's unfathomable grace and contributes nothing to justification about which one could boast before God.* On the contrary, we learn a new subjectivity; in the words of Paul, 'I am crucified to the world and the world is crucified to me!' We learn to sing the dirge of Revelation 18 over the form of this world that is passing away: *sic transit gloria mundi!*"

"Yes, *but!*" Leo interjected. "The kingdom of this world has become the kingdom of our Lord and of His Christ! You say some things well and rightly but then your tone always becomes too extreme! Do not so magnify sinfulness and its effects that you effectively minimize grace and its effects. The gift is *not* like the sin. Surely it is true that we *are continuously exposed to the power of sin still pressing its attacks and are not exempt from a lifelong struggle against the contradiction to God within the selfish desires of the old Adam.* We therefore *also must ask God daily for forgiveness as in the Lord's Prayer, are ever again called to conversion and penance, and are ever again granted forgiveness.* We concede this actual ambiguity of the concrete Christian life, and thus we allow theologically for the persistence of sins in the life of the redeemed. But at the same time we do not minimize the almighty power of grace in baptism that removes sinfulness and in its place pours the grace of the Spirit of God into our souls, renewing us and making us pure. Christ has redeemed us! This is the more salient truth! We are the new creation! What remains of sin in the baptized people of God is and only can be an ember or tinder of wayward desire that under temptation from the world outside the reborn soul can ignite again into the flame of lust. If so, when the Christian comes to her senses, having fallen into the flaming sea of sin, she can swim back to the ark of baptismal grace and purity. Thus there is the second plank provided for us, the plank of penance by which she swims back onto the ark of our salvation."

Luther was annoyed that the conversation that had progressed so well had now circled back to the nature of repentance, the theological issue involved in the attack on indulgences in the Ninety-Five Theses that had provoked the entire controversy. "True and evangelical preaching is to magnify the sins as much as possible that man may develop a fear of God and proper repentance.[7] We do not minimize grace and its effects[8] when we acknowledge the transpersonal nature of sinfulness that has overtaken us in Adam before ever we make a conscious choice to sin. We are born into exile from Eden. We are born children of a fallen humanity. The danger in your way of speaking about sin is that it is reduced to the visible transgressions of individuals readily judged by the law and punished according to human judgment. What is this moralizing but the special wickedness that is the presumption of righteousness by the so-called good people of the world? Have you never read the second chapter of Romans and considered the strange sinfulness of the pious who boast of their goodness, despising the sinner?

"Here is the sober truth of revelation: because of sinfulness inherited from Adam we sin even, if not especially, in our good deeds and pious choices, in that we do them for our own benefit in order to have something to boast about before God. We love God for our sakes, not for God's sake. It is this spiritual sin of the soul that we are to be delivered from, not merely the crude and visible sins of carnality on which you too easily and too mercilessly fixate—as if the evil body made a good soul sin. Friend, it is the other way around! It is the soul blindly captivated by evil that leads the good body into sins!"

"What are you saying?" Leo demanded. "What else have you just done than so exaggerate sin that grace becomes only a footnote? No wonder you feared letting loose the hordes of hell, since you imagine a net from which there is no escape, snaring even, if not especially, those who would escape. What follows from this? Shall we then sin that grace may abound? Shall we stumble in the dark that light may shine? And what kind of fictitious righteousness are you recommending, extrinsically imputed but not inwardly transformative, if good works are made by you into something poisonous, even harmful to salvation? Personal responsibility for sins and capacity for justice is swallowed up in such global pessimism! Pious choices are turned into cunning tricks of the devil! With this kind of doctrine, mark my words, the churches, having become pointless, will soon be empty and no one will have any reason to sustain the struggle of religion in the world!"

Luther was again stopped short at this line of attack about his "unintended" reformation. Surely empty churches and the abandonment of discipleship were not be the intended effect of his reform. Why, to the contrary, he had railed against false security and cheap grace. He had concluded the Ninety-Five Theses with a peroration to discipleship: Christians should be "diligent in following Christ their head through penalties, death and hell, and thus be confident of entering heaven through many tribulations rather than through the false security of peace." But Leo was right that in a sense Luther was the victim again of a certain kind of abstraction, if for a moment he allows Christians to look at themselves outside of Christ who has united with them in baptism, which seems precisely what he allowed in teaching that the Christian is sinful and righteous at the same time. He thus seemed guilty of a blatant contradiction. Which is it? Do Christian look at themselves only in Christ? Or do they also look at themselves outside of Christ? Which is the reality?

If Christians look at themselves outside of their being in Christ, that would mean looking at themselves through the law. In this perspective, Christians indeed recognize that they remain totally sinners. Sin still lives in them, for they repeatedly turn to false gods and do not love God with that undivided love that God requires as their Creator. This contradiction to God is as such truly sin. Looking at themselves through the law, of course, is also seeing how they can look in the skeptical eyes of the world, which hears such fantastic claims about new creation but sees the same old Adam or Eve. In the same way, the world looks upon the Lamb of God and sees a man dying in despair; or looks upon the body and blood on the altar and sees but loaf and cup; or looks upon the Mother of God and sees only a women who is pregnant out of wedlock. The contradiction of which Luther seemed guilty is not a logical failure but a reflection of a conflicted reality in the tension between the already of justification and the not-yet of salvation. As such, all the Christian mysteries are subject to this double perspective, since the Christian is in the world though not of the world, seeing both by the light of nature and by the light of grace, in the perspective of being under the law and in the perspective of being in Christ. Yet seeing the same things in this twofold way does not amount to a mere change in words. A change in perception is a change in reality, since the seer affects what is seen. So also, the believer has what she believes. Only the changed being, the Christian in Christ, is thus capable of this double vision. The world is not capable of this double vision. It perceives only in the light of nature and only from the perspective of the law and therefore sees in the Christian only a change in words, not of reality. In reality, the Christian sees not only with the world and under the law, that he contradicts God in many ways, but also that the enslaving power of sin is broken on the basis of the merit of Christ. *It no longer is a sin that "rules" the Christian for it is itself "ruled" by Christ with whom the justified are bound in faith. In this life, then, Christians can in part lead a just life.* For he suffers now, no longer because of the old fear of punishment, but because of his new love of righteousness.[9] Just so in struggle, indeed in mortal combat, Christ rules over sin in His believers.

This matter of the Christian's double vision was the real problem that Leo was having in understanding Luther's difficult affirmation of "sin ruled" so that the Christian in fact leads a progressively more just life. Luther's precise meaning was that Christ rules over sin in believers when believers look at themselves in Christ, but sin overcomes believers when they look at themselves outside of Christ. This is how Luther took the unsettling teaching of Romans 7 about the divided self, which he attributed to the Christian who lives between baptism as in principle a death to sin in Christ, as discussed in Romans 6, and the glory yet to be revealed in Romans 8, straining forward in eager longing for the revelation of the liberty of the redeemed body of the new creation in fullness and power. Because they live between the times, as Romans 7 depicts, believers have this double vision reflecting the double reality of the apocalyptic battle, wholly sinful and wholly righteous. It is precisely as believers that they are distressed at this conflicted reality of the warfare between the Spirit and flesh that rages in them and cry out for the final victory of Jesus Christ.

85

The body is not yet redeemed. Christians remain bound to the common body where sin reigns unperturbed unless disturbed by the conscientious vocations of the baptized. Bound to the common body, Christians in the world cannot divest from the marketplace, cannot do without the protections of civil justice, cannot eat without predation, nor sleep without nightmares arising from the moral ambiguity that thus attends their highly tensed righteousness in Christ: a conscience at peace with God through our Lord Jesus Christ and the same a conscience troubled in the world by its sinfulness that dwells within and is at work in their own members.

Luther gave title to this Christian art of double vision, *the distinction and right ordering of law and gospel. God's* law, that is, God in the activity of true judge and *God's* gospel, that is, God in the activity of justifier in truth. "Look again," Luther resumed the interchange with Leo, "at how far I am from teaching that the law avails nothing and that Christian righteousness is a legal fiction. What I am trying to bring out is that it is the work of Christ that counts as fulfillment of the law's holy demand for love and thus surpasses the law of God as a judgment upon us who are not so loving. It is His life of obedient faith that is the one, truly good life lived in faith toward His God and Father and in self-giving love of the Spirit for others lesser and unworthy. The backbone of my teaching is that *Christ has fulfilled the law.* Thus, in this fulfillment *by his death and resurrection* He *has overcome it as a way to salvation* now to give Himself as the way, the truth, and the life. Not that he abrogated an antiquated system, but that he fulfilled God's enduring and righteous will and thus surpassed its ministry of condemnation to put into effect the glorious new covenant of grace. Antinomian doctrines claiming my name teach that the law is useless for justification and passé as a result of the revelation of the gracious God in heaven. This is *not* my doctrine, though I must admit that some of my over-the-top rhetoric gave rise to this misunderstanding.[10] At the beginning of my ministry we were frightened at the rustle of leaves, so stricken we were with guilty consciences and the fear of hell. But after the preaching of grace we became Epicureans and human swine. So let it be very clear that *we also confess* with you that *God's commandments retain their validity for the justified and that Christ has by his teaching and example expressed God's will, which is a standard for the conduct of the justified also."*

"I concede the point, dear Luther," Leo said, not without an inward grin at Luther's clear affirmation that justification expresses practically the dogmatic truth of Christ's atoning death in fulfillment of temple and Torah and that the new covenant brought no relaxation of the demand for holiness but rather a radicalization of it. "Just because this is true, while *recognizing his own failures, the believer may yet be certain that God intends his salvation.* No doubt, then, we two in our present purgatory should claim this certainty for ourselves, even though we cannot yet see the way forward. But certainty of God's will for our salvation strengthens us to persevere in this deliberation. Speaking for myself, light has been shed."

"I could not deny what you say, brother, without denying the heart and soul of all that I have believed, taught, and confessed," Luther replied as in an echo of Leo's reflection. "But this *consensus in basic truths of the doctrine of justification must prove itself the life and teachings of our churches. In this respect, there are still questions of varying importance [that] need further clarification. These include, among other topics, the relationship between the Word of God and church doctrine, as well as ecclesiology, ecclesial authority, church unity, ministry, the sacraments, and the relation between justification and social ethics. We are convinced that the consensus we have reached offers a solid basis for this clarification."*

"Very well, then," Leo replied, "let us proceed."

"But I am hungry," Luther objected. "Aren't you?"

"Yes, to think of it, I am hungry. In fact, I am famished." The portly pope, like the portly doctor of theology, loved his food and drink, both temporal and spiritual.

"I wonder. Do we get fed around here?"

"I wonder...too." Leo's drawn-out response indicated that he really meant it. It *was* a perplexing state of being they were in. They had already learned that the Great and Heavenly Banquet awaited them whenever they could leave their present place together to sit at table side by side. But they were not there yet. Was there now no provision for them still on the way? Or could one eat now while the other goes without? Or eat

87

to the exclusion of the other? Or is perhaps purgatory a time of Eucharist fasting? The last thought made Leo shudder.

"Perhaps we are meant to fast."

"Yes, perhaps," Luther assented, having at the moment nothing better to say. What a twist, a consensus on justification that did not satisfy but only made them hungrier!

EUCHARIST AND SACRIFICE

BACKSTORY

As rapidly as the controversy over indulgences was eclipsed by the question of authority in the church, and as quickly as defense of the merchandizing of indulgences collapsed before Luther's withering critique, a new target came into focus in his polemic against "papist" trafficking in sacred things. He called this new target "the sacrifice of the mass," meaning the ritual practice of a spiritual or "unbloody" sacrifice on the altar *at a time when people received communion rarely and viewing the elevated host,* or adoration of the reserved host, *was seen [as] a powerful form of contact with Christ as a sort of substitute for receiving Communion.*[1] In this development, it can hardly be denied (also on the Catholic side in the reforms of Vatican II) that the mass had become a spectacle to be observed rather than a meal to be shared and just so a *koinonia* in the body and blood of Christ, the risen One who had been crucified. That latter would indicate that at its heart the Christian assembly is a communion and that the assembly of these assemblies is a communion of communions—an alternative theology of the visible unity of the universal church amidst the plurality of local churches. Be that as it may, what was even worse, for

Luther, was that in the process of making the Eucharist a spectacle rather than a communion, the precious and unmerited gift of God in the communion was turned into a meritorious offering to God.

Yet this critique by Luther was not quite fair or even consequent with his own theological understanding of the gift of God that consisted in Christ's sacrifice on the cross. The idea in the sacrifice of the mass was that of the divinely provided Lamb of God (cf. Genesis 22:8). As the bread and wine are miraculously turned by God into the body and blood of Christ, they are given by God to be offered back to God as a proper propitiation for, or satisfaction of, divine anger on the poor sinners who assembled to witness the spiritual sacrifice. God thus graciously provides the means of atonement in the sacrifice of the mass. Sorting out just how Luther disagrees with this way of understanding God's gift as God's sacrifice is a matter of some subtlety, especially when Catholic theologians clarify that the sacrifice of the mass is a *re-presentation* of once-and-for-all Calvary, not, as alleged, a *repetition* of it. As a re-presentation, it does just what Luther required: it proclaims the Lord's death for us until He comes again. It does not amplify or supplement with meritorious human performance the once-for-all sacrifice of the Lamb of God, which as such is all-sufficing for human salvation.

All the same, this belief, as Luther understood it, that the "mass is a good work and a sacrifice," he railed, "has brought an endless host of other abuses in its train, so that the faith of this sacrament has become utterly extinct and the holy sacrament has been turned into mere merchandise, a market, and a profit-making business."[2] This allegation is borne by the facts. A lucrative business in the saying and selling of masses for the living and the dead had in fact developed, as attested by the many, today little-used side-altars in European churches where priests quickly whispered the liturgies and performed the sacrifices in the absence of a congregational *koinonia* to the benefit of donors not present or their suffering loved ones away in purgatory.

An accoutrement of this practice that further offended Luther was how it reinforced a strong distinction between clergy as the priests who offered the sacrifice, and the laity, who witnessed the offering on their behalf, by withholding the cup from the latter. But the sacrament belongs to the entire Christian people, Luther argued, and the ministers of it are their servants, not lords, just as needy as those not ordained to this service.

Another problem for Luther was that the value of the mass as an efficacious sacrifice relied theologically on a doctrine formulated in terms taken from Aristotle's philosophical vocabulary, which distinguished between the outer, visible appearance of bread and wine and the underlying, invisible substance, which latter was said to be miraculously changed from that of bread into that of the body of Christ as the priest recited the *Hoc est corpus meum* ("This is my body," corrupted into the magical incantation "hocus pocus" and used as a taunt against Catholic "superstition"). This marvel was thought necessary to provide efficacy to the sacrifice. The offering of mere bread and wine could hardly propitiate for sins offending God; nothing less than the body and blood of Christ would suffice for the sacrifice to avail and actually take away the anger of God upon the sin of the world. God's grace was seen, not as theological liberals imagine in abandoning anger as inconsistent with love; why would a *crucified* Christ be needed for *that*? But the Father's grace consists in His provision of this precious Lamb, Christ the Son, whom He loved but did not spare and gave up for us all in that infinitely precious sacrifice that would satisfy divine justice and so still divine anger.

Luther was no theological liberal. But neither was he a conservative. He was, rather, consistently Pauline. He is ever probing the meaning of a statement like that in 2 Corinthians 5:21: "God caused the one who didn't know sin to be sin for our sake so that through him we could become the righteousness of God." Luther agreed that atonement was necessary. Yet Luther did not understand atonement quite like Anselm of Canterbury had in his classic treatise of early scholasticism, *Why God Became Man*. Briefly put, the problem of atonement was defined by Anselm as that of an infinite debt incurred by those who had offended the honor of God as Creator and Governor of the world. The offense is not about God's private ego, so to say. The wrath of God is not private rage but the public love of God against what is against love. What is at issue in God's controversy with the world is moral injury inflicted on the creation of the Creator by

91

sin and the moral need for reparative justice for creation to continue to its goal of blessedness. Only the creature who owes the debt can repay the debt, but only God can fund the repayment. Hence, God became human to accomplish this restorative justice.

The sinless God-Man had no obligation to die. But freely he sacrificed Himself, accruing an infinitude of surplus credit, so to speak. Nor did the sinless God-Man need this surplus for Himself, but He graciously makes it available to those in need through the sacraments of the church. Thus Anselm: Christ crucified by his active obedience voluntarily bore human punishment that He Himself did not deserve. He is a punishment-bearer who can and does fund others in need of relief so that they, too, can justly avoid punishment by restoring justice in availing themselves of His gift of merit to pay their debts.

Luther does not disagree with Anselm at all about the need of atonement. He differs rather dramatically, however, in regarding Christ, not as a punishment-bearer who delivers from punishment by supplying merit to those in need, but as a sin-bearer who takes away the sin of the world: "So our sins must be borne by the wounded Christ rather than in our own consciences. For in Christ our sins are dead, but in us they live."[3] By His solidarity with sinners even to death on a cross, Christ victorious in love leaves the sin of the world behind, dead and buried in the tomb. Thus he enables believers, relieved of this guilt and the burden to atone, to endure the cross and grave on the way to final blessedness. The good news of atonement for Luther, you might say, is that sinners get to die with Christ in principle and in power by their baptism into His death. Because of Christ's atonement, God is now "satisfied with a contrite heart."[4] For this contrite heart marks the transformation of desire: "Beyond all satisfaction is the satisfaction of love, for by means of punishment God himself requires nothing else except that love should be perfected."[5] This transformation of desire is what demarcates the love of Adam from love in Christ: "What the former dreads, the latter longs for. And since each of them is motivated by an entirely different desire, what is for the former the greatest dread is to the latter the highest gain and joy."[6] In Christ they get to die as Adam and get to arise as believers to newness of life; they are sustained on their pilgrim way in this new existence by feeding on the body of Christ given for them. For Luther, all other food that creatures eat gets turned into them. But the eating of this blessed food turns believers into the body of Christ.

For all his polemics, then, Luther's disagreement on this crucial point in the understanding of gift and sacrifice was subtle. He hardly denied that God provided the Lamb or that the Lamb provided was needed. The sacrifice on Calvary "for us and our salvation," he taught, was not repeated but re-presented in the mass. Thus he did not deny the true Presence of the body of Christ in the sacrament for believers to eat; in fact, he emphatically upheld it, provided it was understood as a gift to God's people in need, clergy too, rather than a meritorious work of the church's clergy on behalf of others in need.

In denying the concept of "transubstantiation," he denied not "the Presence" but the philosophical conceptuality in which "the Presence" was articulated: "I at last found rest for my conscience in the...view, namely, that it is real bread and real wine, in which Christ's real flesh and blood are present in no other way and to no less a degree than the others assert them to be under their accidents."[7] Theologically, if not philosophically then, Luther would rather drink Christ's blood with papists than mere wine with symbolists or memorialists: "What really mattered to him was that the body of Christ was present in the Lord's Supper through the power of the Word. Christ's Word [of promise, 'This is my body *given for you*'] brings together the elements and Christ."[8] But this nuance (which turns on Luther's differentiating of theology as the Spirit's new language in the light of grace from philosophy as humanity's old language in the light of nature) was lost on contemporary Catholics. It was lost on them thanks once again to the polemical writing of the German papists. Johannes Eck blamed radical rejection of the Lord's Supper among diverse other dissenters on Luther personally: "We must acknowledge as Luther's sons the iconoclasts, the sacramentarians, the Capernaites, the Neo-Hussites, and their descendants, the Anabaptist, the Neo-Epicureans who declare the soul to be mortal, the enthusiasts, also the Neo-Cerinthians who deny the deity of Christ... destroy the churches, demolish the altars, trample upon the most holy Eucharist."[9]

If it is also true, as Luther himself tacitly conceded when he acknowledged the papists' intention to affirm the presence of the Lord's body "under the accidents," that *the concept of transubstantiation, for its part, is intended as a confession and preservation of the Mystery-character of the Eucharistic presence... not as an explanation of* how *this change occurs*, then, Luther's position and that of the Catholic *tradition must not longer be regarded as opposed in a way that leads to separation.* With this, be it carefully noted, comes a recognition of a definite pluralism in theological explication. This is not a vulgar pluralism but a critical one. It is a recognition of the finitude and particularity of all theological explication, not license for speculation that no longer transparently intends to preserve the mysteries while communicating them as gospel.

Indeed, it is important to see that because Christ's body given for the believer is what "really mattered" to Luther he felt forced to make a categorical differentiation. He had to differentiate between the sacrament as Christ's testament of his self-offering to the benefit of the faithful from the faithful's sacrifice of praise in return. Eucharistic sacrifice was a long-standing and entrenched liturgical tradition; as with the practice of indulgences, Luther historically and critically traced the language of sacrifice in the mass liturgy back to the blessing in early Christianity on the bread and wine brought forward with other gifts collected at the mass for distribution to the poor and homebound. As with indulgences, this innocent and indeed praiseworthy practice of charity over time transposed into the religion business. So Luther felt impelled to assert a disjunction: "These two things—mass and prayer, sacrament and work, testament and sacrifice—must not be confused; for the one comes from God to us through the ministration of the priest and demands our faith, the other proceeds from our faith to God through the priest and demands his hearing. The former descends, the latter ascends."[10]

In fact Luther's description of the two motions of the Eucharistic liturgy here is *apt*. There *are* dynamic movements of descent and ascent in it that are inherited from the early Christians. One could put it this way in language from Paul's Letter to the Galatians, which Luther so dearly treasured. The Father sends "his Son, born through a woman, and born under the Law" (Gal 4:4-5). By joining Himself innocent and in the power of the Spirit to those guilty and accursed in His act of descending love, Christ unites the faithful to Himself so that with Him, in the power of the same Spirit, they return the glory to God the Father: "God sent the Spirit of his Son into our hearts, crying, 'Abba, Father!'" (Gal 4:6). So *in Eucharistic worship the church participates in a unique way in the life of the Trinity: In the power of the Holy Spirit, called down upon the gifts and the worshipping community, believers have access to the glorified flesh and blood of Christ the Son as our food and are brought in union with him and with each other to the Father.* If that is right, the *traditional Catholic emphasis on the movement* ad Patrem *(to the Father) and the Lutheran emphasis on the movement* ad populum *(to the people)* is not so much a necessary disjunction as it is a reflection of a tragic mutual deficit in trinitarianism. We see here a reciprocating deficit in the trinitarian understanding of the distinct but inseparable roles of the Son and the Spirit in moving the people of God to receive and to give, to believe and to love, to trust and to obey. And this tragic bifurcation touches upon the central event of the ecclesia gathered to word and sacrament.

All that is explicitly lacking in Luther's description of these movements of descent and ascent is the trinitarian articulation of God such that grace is manifest and effective as *both* the descending love of the Son in His self-offering for us on Calvary once and for all, and thus also now to us in the Eucharist, *and* the ascending love of the Spirit who unites us to Christ by the common eating and drinking, so that in Him we are lifted up to lift up our hearts to the Lord, offering ourselves in praise to the Father. Lacking this trinitarian articulation at this specific place (though not elsewhere), Luther argued himself into a corner, which in the course of time caused the Holy Spirit virtually to disappear in Lutheranism as nugatory, as a fifth wheel who did no real theological work, who became nothing but a pious gloss on the human actions of believers.[11] Indeed, if we feel forced to treat Christian life as the merely human response to grace in order to preserve a christomonistic conception of monergistic

95

grace, the Holy Spirit becomes nugatory, while human reception and piety and discipleship and doxology steadily shed their inhibitions and take on center stage. This trinitarian truncation, exacerbated by anti-Catholic polemics, would thus have devastating consequences for Luther's followers through the centuries. Who needs to go to church, or commune, if the human response to God's word of grace is my own private affair, in my own competence and jurisdiction? Only those who go to church in order to worship—this subtle idolatry cannot be soft-pedaled—their own piety and discipleship and doxology! Likewise the presupposition of the entire theology of the Eucharist in Christ's atonement has been forfeited. Deliverance from the wrath to come has to do with God's public controversy with the world run amuck in sin and violence. But the private Protestant Christian of today is sure that he or she will go to heaven, no matter what the church says, since God loves good people, leaving those who feel the need for it to come to church to celebrate their goodness.

But the *decisive point* in recovering the trinitarian understanding of God as articulated and perpetually rehearsed in the Eucharistic liturgy is *not that what is past is called to mind, but that the Lord calls his people into his presence and confronts them with his salvation. In this creative act of God, the salvation event from the past becomes the offer of salvation for the present and the promise of salvation for the future.* It is as members so joined to the body of Christ that they are equipped for nonconformity to this dying world, transformed for service in the body, made responsible to God for His creation in travail at the new creation aborning. Thus the trinitarian Eucharist proffers a *holy secularity*, precisely not the abject blessing (whether on the Right or on the Left) of *secularism* that prevails among today's desacramentalized Protestants.

CONVERSATION

"Can we eat only if we are holy?" Luther broke a rather long silence, if only to distract himself from the hunger pangs.

"Holy things for holy people," Leo replied. "The doors! The doors!" he continued, reminding Luther of the early church's practice after the liturgy of the word to send out seekers and even catechumens not yet baptized, so that only the baptized would receive the holy meal. "We are not to cast pearls before swine. That is why we have sacramental penance prior to admission at the Lord's Table. Those who receive must be restored to a state of grace in baptismal purity."

The last statement hit Luther hard. He had been of a double mind on the practice of private confession and absolution. He had denied its special sacramental status as penance but urged its retention as a pastoral practice. Indeed, he said that when he urged people to go to private confession he was only urging them to be Christians. But he had emphatically rejected it as a legalistic prerequisite to communion, which, he alleged, tyrannized and/or infantilized consciences. But when he saw face-to-face the ignorance and scorn that prevailed among nominal Christians, he, too, maintained that "anyone who will not believe the gospel, live according to it, and do what a Christian ought to do should enjoy none of its benefits." They were to be excluded, then, from the communion. So he was of a double mind: "We want nothing to do with compulsion. However, if anyone does not hear and heed our preaching and warning, we shall have nothing to do with such a person who ought not have any part of the gospel."[12]

Was this a wish or a command or just a dodge?

"All the Christian life is nothing but a perpetual return to baptism," Luther now said, trying to steer Leo's remark in a better direction. "From baptism day to the day of the resurrection, we are daily to slay the old Adam and rise up afresh to newness of life. It is not good enough to be born again once. We must be born again every new day! The one who lives this way is in the state of grace that cannot be lost by venial or trivial sins or even by our abiding sinfulness, if it be ruled by Christ and thus constrained. In this state of grace, then, private confession should be an aid and comfort in sustaining this way of life."

"I don't understand you, Luther," the pope replied. "When we are in a state of grace we are spotless, holy, and undefiled. As such we commune. Indeed, only as such dare we commune with the holy God."

"Ah," Luther sighed. "You are thinking of holiness again like a law-yer or a philosopher, not like a theologian trained in the Scriptures. Ho-liness does not mean that we cease to be mortal and sinful people, for the saints—note well, I say, the *saints*!—daily must pray, 'Forgive us our debts,' just as we saints must each someday die." Luther was speaking out of habit, not realizing for the moment that he and Leo were both dead. "Holiness means that in spite of mortality and sin, God's makes us His own people, calls us out of the dying world and unto Himself, pledges Himself to be our faithful God in spite of our recurring faithlessness. We are sanctified by God's loving regard for us and effective calling of us, not because we have otherwise acquired holiness like a quality that substan-tially adheres to us."

"I see," said Leo, now himself annoyed. "We have come back to that sticking point between us, your assertion of the contradiction in terms, 'sinner and righteous at the same time,' as if it were an intelligible claim to truth and not gibberish to which no one can actually say yes, or no."

"A contradiction," Luther rejoined, "must be a contradiction not only in terms but also in sense if it is to be regarded as fallacious. I have said that we are wholly sinful in the perspective of divine law but holy righ-teous in the perspective of the gospel of the righteousness of God in Christ that avails precisely for those who are sinners and the ungodly under the law. And you know that I do not intend this paradox as some flat-footed and static resignation to Christian existence as a being of perpetual equiv-ocity. We are sinners; we are 'this world' that 'resists and even rejects the reality of the love of God which is bestowed upon it in Jesus Christ. This world has fallen under the sentence which God passes on all enmity to Christ. It is engaged in a life and death struggle with the church. And yet it is the task of the Church that she shall impart to precisely this world its reconciliation with God and that she shall open its eyes to the reality of the love of God, against which it is blindly raging. In this way it is also, and indeed especially, it is the lost and sentenced world that is incessantly drawn into the event of Christ.'[13] We are sinners; that is true. But we are sinners beloved and forgiven and renewed in Christ. Both statements are

98

true. Whoever knows this in faith hungers and thirsts for the bread of heaven that sustains such contested faith on its pilgrim way."

"So," Leo nodded, "we could say 'holy things for holy people' speaking to those who know that they are poor sinners in need of nurture and healing?"

"Yes," Luther replied. "Blessed are those who mourn, for they shall be comforted."

"Ah," signed Leo, "blessed griefwork again!"

"But all the more so holy are those sinners who believe in Christ as their true brother and friend. These are holy in the biblical sense, as those called out of darkness into marvelous light."

"I hunger for that marvelous light; I thirst for the great and Heavenly Banquet. My appetite is whetted. I am ready to eat! The Eucharist *as sacramental participation in the glorified body and blood of Christ is a pledge that our life in Christ will be eternal, our bodies will rise, and the present world is destined for transformation, in the hope of uniting us in communion with the saints of all ages now with Christ is heaven.* I think now especially of my beloved father, Lorenzo—the Magnificent, they called him. He warned me against the sins for which I am now suffering.[14] I want to see him, not only out of profound filial love and piety, but also for a penitential reason. I have to—I want—to tell him how he was right to warn me. I don't want too much to see Savonarola; he still makes my flesh crawl! But I would also see Pico della Mirandola who also warned me.[15] I am seeing now that heaven is both fulfillment of creation and this eschaton of judgment, this reconciliation of all conflicts. Oh, what yet bars us from attaining?"

Luther answered, "Is it not the simple fact that what bars us is that we cannot see how we shall enter together, indeed *only* together?"

"Luther, I can grant that you intend to affirm the Presence in the Eucharist. You can grant that by mass-sacrifice I mean to re-present the once for all sacrifice of Calvary, Christ for us. The *Catholic doctrine of the mass, let me say emphatically, is the making present of the sacrifice of the cross. It is not a repetition of this sacrifice and adds nothing to its saving significance. It is an affirmation and not a questioning of the uniqueness and full value of Christ's sacrifice on the cross.* I can also grant that you intend union with Christ who sacrificed Himself for us as the saving truth expressed in teaching justification by faith alone in Christ alone. You can grant that union with Christ includes the gift of His Spirit so the church's prayer and thanksgiving is not some private and autonomous human response to God's word but God's own response to God's word, the Spirit whom we invoke and who comes to sweep together our hearts up to the Lord. Does that agreement on the Eucharist as both Christ for us and Christ in us not suffice? Can you not now return to Mother Church so that together we can leave this cold place and at least eat together at the table in the kingdom of God?"

"I would like very much to say *satis est*, yes, that suffices. But, Leo, I have never left Mother Church, which bears and begets every believer through the word of God. Nor have I ever denied that Mother Church exists in the Church of Rome. On the contrary, I have insisted that all good things have come to us from the church in Rome. Do not confuse *me*, brother Leo, as did those papist flatterers in Germany who caught your ear. Do *not* confuse *me* with those who deny the substance of the faith that was passed onto to us from *you*!"[16]

"I have learned not to do so in this time together. But what then still stands in the way of your return to Mother Church?"

Luther could barely contain himself. "Return? Again, I say, I never left! I was kicked out, betrayed, and burned at the stake!"

"Oh, yes. That's right."

"Can't you admit that?"

"Privately, yes. It was my personal sin to have rushed to judgment in your case, distracted as I was at the time.[17] It is evident to me now that I judged falsely as a result. In fact, I am sorry, Martin, not just on account of the punishment that has put me in the place with you—indeed, I am grateful now for that punishment that led me by the light of truth to see my fault. But I am sorry, blessedly grieved, for the wrong I did to you and in so doing to the church of Christ."

"For me personally it is a little thing to forgive you. But as to the damage done to the church, the repair should be public."

"Well, perhaps, but it is too late for that," Leo conceded.

"If God forgives real, not fictitious sinners—Peter who denied and Paul who persecuted—and restored them to the church, it is never too late. Isn't that why we are here together in purgatory?"

"It would seem so. But then why are you here?"

"Ironically enough," Luther reflected, "I see that I am guilty of the same sin—a rush to judgment. I never considered that my chosen form of communication—the paradox—could be a hindrance to understanding. Sometimes I delighted in my obscurity, concealing a certain spiritual pride and sense of intellectual superiority over those outsiders who could not understand the sense of my paradoxes. Even the sin for which I am most guilty—the rush to judgment in identifying you as antichrist—was intended as a paradox. I took the Apostle's statement that antichrist takes his seat in the temple of God to mean that antichrist could only arise within the *true* temple of God. But few people, not even insiders, got the intended irony."

"There is no room for word games now," Leo said. "With plain truth plainly stated comes reconciliation. We must be clear about things. We must discern what still stands in the way."

"Very well, then. Can we really talk, as you have, about a *return* to Mother Church? When you excommunicated me, and I felt driven to identify you as antichrist *within* the church, you did not drive out a heretic but rather rendered the seamless robe of Christ. After that the Catholic Church became a confessional church like all the others, each claiming to be the true church. We are *all* since then fragments, torn members of a bleeding, even dying, body of Christ. You, too, who so proudly takes up the great word, *catholic*, turns it into the party slogan of a partisan denomination alongside other partisan denominations. Think of it, 'Roman Catholic,' a kind of oxymoron, if the sense is that one particular local church claims to represent the universality of the local churches."

Leo recognized Luther's logic. "You are trying to play my own card against me. It was we Catholics in particular who warned against the multiplication of churches that would follow from your turn to a principle of private judgment of religious truth. We in particular have upheld the principle of catholic comprehensiveness and universality."

Luther could not deny the consequence; it was already a fact that he tacitly acknowledged when he insisted that Leo not lump him together with other dissenters, his supposed "sons," as Eck had done. He sputtered, "Let us return to the subject under discussion. What remains in the way is, at least in part for me, a christological concern. Even if you clarify that transubstantiation is an attempt to express and preserve the mystery of the Eucharistic union of Christ's body with the visible elements, not to explain rationalistically how it occurs, and even if I see that the intention here is not to repeat and multiply sacrifices but to re-present the once for all and all-sufficient sacrifice of Golgotha, I still have a worry that the conceptuality you choose to use misleads us."

Leo nodded for Luther to continue.

"What I mean is this. The Eucharistic union is analogous to the personal or hypostatic union of divine and human natures in the person of the Incarnate Son. Now, note, an analogy is *not* an identity but is a certain similarity in relations. As the bread is to the body, so the humanity of Christ is to His deity. That is the analogy. The difference is that the union of Christ's body and the loaf is *not* a personal union, as in the union of humanity and deity in Christ's person. In the incarnation the eternal Son of God personally takes to Himself human nature from the Virgin Mary and makes it His very own humanity henceforth and forever, so that all that the Son does and ever will do, He does by virtue of this personal union with our humanity. But in the Lord's Supper, the union is not perpetual in this way, only temporary; nor is it personal, as it is a union of body to loaf, not person to nature."

"What is my concern, you wonder, in bringing up these fine points of christological doctrine? It is *not* that these technical points as such stand in the way of our *koinonia* in the body and blood of Christ. Rather, I raise these difficult points to get at a deeper and thus more obscure divergence between us. My concern is that the model of transubstantiation, by which the substance of the bread is annihilated to make way for the substance of the body of Christ, suggests by analogy a certain kind of docetism. Docetism, from the Greek verb *dokeo*, 'to seem,' was the first Christian heresy, alleging that Jesus only *seemed* to be human, only *appeared* to die on the cross. Analogously, transubstantiation as a conceptual model suggests that the bread only appears to be bread and that we only seem to eat bread. If the analogies can run up and down the great chain of being, then, my concern is that here it is inevitably suggested that the divinity of Christ really supplants—indeed annihilates and replaces—His humanity. Thus for all practical purposes—and what else is the Lord's Supper than practical Christology?—it is not our connection with that particular human being, Jesus of Nazareth, who brought God near to sinners who is thought to save, but in fact *any* old sacramental or incarnational contact with deity."[18]

Leo needed time to take all this in. But he was disturbed by the precise point at which Luther said that the analogy between the incarnation and the Eucharist breaks down, implying that the sacramental union was only temporary. Could the bread that had become the blessed vehicle and sacred vessel of the body of Christ ever cease to be sanctified? Could it be thrown to the birds or left for the mice or tossed into the garbage? The idea immediately repulsed him in the same way that Luther was repulsed at the docetism suggested by the concept of transubstantiation. Isn't it, Leo wondered, just another docetism that treats the blessed bread and wine as nothing but ordinary bread and wine? His hunger pangs, now, cried to him all the more.

CHURCH AND MAGISTERIUM

BACKSTORY

E ven if purgatory is invisible and a matter of faith, Christianity is visible. In fact purgatory is a belief about the true but hidden nature of visible Christianity. This visibility is the fact of the church in the world. This fact exists, however, because adherents believe something quite distinctive about themselves, and apart from this distinctive belief they would disband and dissipate and finally disappear from the visibility of human history. It is hardly controversial, moreover, to identify in a broad way what it is chiefly that they believe about themselves. They believe that they are under a commission, *mandated to carry out a mission in which the church participates in God's activity in the world by evangelization, worship, service of humanity and care for creation.*[1] We can stipulate that this much is visible, a positive fact accessible to all and not in itself controversial: in Christianity people gather, organize, and act in accordance with their peculiar mandate as they in faith understand it. One can thus see such in the mere light of nature from the rhetoric and the icons, the practices and rituals, the preaching and teaching that the phenomenon in the world that is the Christian church is, despite all internal variety and diversity, here and not there, something occupying definite space and time. What is not visible, however—what remains even if not especially to believers a matter of faith and not sight—is that this visible church is also what it would in all these visible ways *signify*: the people of God, the body of Christ, and the temple of the Spirit. These convictions articulate Christian faith; they are articles of faith.

While Christianity as a visible phenomenon in the world is subject to study by any and all human sciences, as also from perspectives not informed by Christian faith, and while such study of Christianity in the light of nature is often quite revealing,[2] the internal and interested study of Christianity that is concerned for the truth of its mandate and the purity of its mission belongs to the ecclesial discipline of theology. Theology is a function of the church.[3] What disciplinary difference does this make from the human sciences? Here the sign is not taken as the absence of the thing signified but as its presence, with only the proviso that this unification of sign and thing signified is a gift and work of the God of grace, given as an event where and when it pleases God. Theology is knowledge of God who gives and ecclesiology is that knowledge of God concerning the Spirit's gifts that are God's people, Christ's body, and the Spirit's temple.

Theologically, then, the church is in its entire existence a sign of the saving will of God, who desires that all people be saved and come to see the truth; just so the church remains constantly subject to the Lord, and salvation remains a gift of God, even in the work of the church. The double vision of the Christian thus applies here as well. The visible church is a sign that is believed against appearances, as Abraham believed against the appearance of his and his wife's aged bodies that the promised child would be born to them (Rom 4). In this sense that faith already has in anticipation what it believes is yet to come, that faith is the substance of things hoped for and the conviction of things not seen (Heb 11), the sign of the church unifies with the thing signified, as it pleases God. This begins in the life of the church itself when against appearances to the contrary the church sustains this belief about itself, namely, that it truly is this divinely given sign to the world of the saving will of God. This is, however, the perpetual trial of ecclesial faith. For this Christian belief in the one, holy,

106

catholic, and apostolic church, as characterized by the Nicene Creed, is not necessarily or automatically or impersonally the case, even for adherents. Then it would be a matter of sight, believing the evidence of one's own eyes, not faith believing the promises of God. Thus the wistful old joke still has traction, "Jesus promised us the kingdom of God. What we got was the church," so that the more one believes in the church the more one suffers from it.

What we got in the church is a visible sign of the saving kingdom of God, which awaits the fullness of this thing signified. Theologians have taken to calling this peculiar ambivalence of a sign that partially, incompletely, or occasionally unifies with things signified by way of faith's anticipation *prolepsis*. The Apostle expresses prolepsis precisely when he says of the church's central rite of the new covenant, "For as often as we eat of this bread and drink of this cup we proclaim the Lord's death until he comes again." The *already* of ecclesial participation or *koinonia* in the death of Christ juxtaposes with the *not yet* of its full participation in the resurrection of Christ: it has faith and the Spirit as a "down payment." It does not yet have full possession, as a true sign of what is yet to come.

A profound temptation to unbelief within the church about the church thus arises and takes subtle form in the apparently humble and pious interpretation that the sign merely points away from itself to the thing signified, that is, to some utopia or "Platonic Republic" that exists only in the dreams of idealists or in the otherworldly mind of God, not in the cranky grandma who the priest never visits enough nor the imperious business man who pays the congregation's budget and expects a return on investment! Catholics have often interpreted Lutheran affirmations of the "spiritual" nature of the "spiritual community," that is, the Spirit's gathering of those called out (ec-clesia) by the gospel, in this Platonizing way. Truth be told, not a few of Luther's self-proclaimed followers have Platonized his teaching in this way and others. But in point of fact Luther himself knew better and resisted that line of thinking.

He spoke not of the invisibility of the church as an idea, but as the hiddenness of the church in the world, thus as the church as an island of hope in a world that treats as real only what is visibly present. This critical

107

distance in treating Christian faith in the church is necessary to sustain the church as hope when hope can be crushed by the total identification of the sign and the thing signified: "Sacramental penance is only external and presupposes inward penance without which it has no value," Luther wrote in expositing the Spirit's lifelong repentance in distinction from the "second plank" rite that had evolved in Christendom; "sacramental penance can be a sham, inward penance cannot exist unless it is true and sincere."[4]

Short, then, of a flat-footed and undialectical identification of the church as the coming kingdom of God, there *are* powerful reasons for succumbing to the temptation to dualize the church as an empty sign of a reality quite other than itself. The reason that this temptation to dualize the sign and the thing signified presses hard is that veils of ambiguity cover the church as sign of the saving reign of God to come from plain sight in nature's light. Moreover, these veils of ambiguity are two and not one. Indeed, what is important to see for the ecumenical future is that the veil does not consist *only* in the all too evident appearances of sin, betrayal, and corruption in the life of the church. Certainly that veil of scandal and hypocrisy grabs our attention easily—yet all too easily, if we would think in this way to be first in casting stones. A pastor tells the story that could probably be repeated a million times of visiting an individual who had occasionally come to the church. When the pastor invited her to take instruction and become a member, she replied, "Oh, Pastor, I like you very much. But I just couldn't stand associating with all those hypocrites." The pastor cleverly replied, "I'll tell you what. Join the church and you and me together, we'll take care of all those hypocrites!" Her bluff called, she never showed her face in the church again. There are few greater hypocrisies than calling out the hypocrisies of others. The church is a hospital for sinners, including the hypocrites who all are in some aspect or degree, not a fortress of the perfect.

So there is, on the contrary, a profound reason for *affirming* this kind of veil that proceeds from the consensus on justification. Believers who know that they are included in spite of their sin, betrayal, and corruption on account of Christ who has befriended them, cannot take offense when the same sins that beset them also manifest in others. Rather they bear with the offender, even while calling the offender to the same repentance in which they struggle against their own sins in the power of Spirit-conduced repentance. The forgiven sinner bears with the sinning sister or brother, fleeing or separating in extremity if need be, but sighing for the final deliverance of both offended and offender that comes with the promised consummation. This ambiguity of patiency in love is not easily understood by the unbelieving world that sees in it not the forbearance of charity in eschatological hope but only compromise and hypocrisy. It cannot in fact see otherwise, as *in the very same sense* it sees only the defeat of a deluded dreamer on the cross. But the patiency of love bears all things, believes all things, and hopes all thing, as Paul attests in that epistle addressed to his most troubled congregation in Corinth; and this reality of Christ hidden in the midst of sinful people who learn to own one another as Christ has owned them is what is not yet visible to the unbelieving world.

This *hiddenness* of the community holy to God on account of His calling by the gospel in spite of persisting sinfulness is *proper*, then, to the pilgrim church still on the way, living in the light of grace not yet of glory. "Your life is *hidden* with Christ in God" (Col 3:3)—that is, "The whole creation waits breathless with anticipation for the *revelation* of God's sons and daughters" (Rom 8:19). To be sure, if we depart from the hard-earned consensus on justification, we are not merely *tempted* to dualize the sign and the thing signified in ecclesiology. We are *forced* to dualize because the manifest contradiction between wholly sinful Christianity in the world and the wholly righteous children of God in Christ is otherwise unbearable. It *is* unbearable, a cross to be fled in horror, unless we see by faith Christ in our midst, who eats and drinks with sinners and tax collectors so that we, too, may patiently bear with one another. Lacking this particular belief about the presence of Christ in service to sinful people, not only are we forced to dualize, but also we dualize self-righteously and schismatically, accusing others of the same hypocrisy that these others see in us. But if we sustain the *dynamic* understanding of the Christian as righteous and sinner at the same time, that is, *on the way* to the victory of righteousness at the consummation, we progress step by painful step as the Spirit prods

109

toward the hope of righteousness. We progress just because we are already regarded as righteous in Christ, this divine regard and good pleasure being the sure foundation and not the uncertain hope of Christian and ecclesial existence. If this consensus on justification holds and applies to Christian life together as church, then the problem of ecclesial fragmentation or disunity appears in another light altogether. It appears now as a trinitarian deficit.

Hence, the persistence of sin in the life of the redeemed is not the only or even chief reason that believers themselves are tempted to dualize the sign and the thing signified in matters ecclesial. Rather, it is because the church in divine reality is not one thing but three. And seeing *in faith* how these three signs of the divine reality hang together as one thing signified *by God* is the outstanding ecumenical theological challenge to ecclesial self-understanding that has yet to be fully engaged, let alone satisfied. We are all to this extent heterodox. Orthodoxy is an intention, not an achievement. The Spirit's work is still under way.

The church is at the same time the Spirit's merciful hospital for sinners, the sanctified agency of Christ in the world, and the Father's ancient promise of blessing, the coming beloved community for all nations, the new creation, the pilgrim people of God safe on Jordan's shore, arrived and at peace in the promised land, the blessed Israel of God. It is all these diverse things at once and cannot be any one of them well except in circulating relations to the other dimensions of its existence. For the God of the gospel grants to the church's members *their sharing in the triune divine life as God's own people, as the body of the risen Christ, and as the temple of the Spirit.* When any of these three dimensions of the church's existence in the life of God is privileged to the exclusion of the others, such distortion arises that believers themselves can only save face by dualizing their broken and distorted sign from the thing it signifies. So it happened, for example, in Lutheranism when the righteousness of faith was taken to be solely a matter of divine regard separable from the union with Christ in the joyful exchange which this imputation signified. Or, for another example, so it happened in Catholicism when the fidelity promised to the assembly was secured as the hierarchy over against the people summoned and equipped by baptism to test the spirits to see whether they are of God. These sorry moves are not of faith so much as desperation.

Even as the coming ecumenical church learns to hold these three dimensions of the church's life in God together in a living circulation, mirroring the distinct persons and associated works of the Father, the Son, and the Holy Spirit, the unification of the sign and the thing signified is given *ubi et quando Deo visum est,* "where and when it pleases God," thus *in an anticipatory fashion or proleptically.* This "eschatological reserve" ever reminds that even at its best, the church's life can only and ever be received as a gift, not claimed as possession, believed and not seen.

The church is first of all a hospital for sinners, as Martin and Leo have been brought together to realize in their purgatorial suffering—above all, their suffering of one another in the patiency of faith that is learning to love and hope for love's victory. *The communion in Christ into which human beings are called endures also in death and judgment. It becomes complete as, though the pain over failure in earthly life persists, persons come with their love to give the perfect response to God.* This blessed griefwork finishes out the bearing of one another's burdens begun in the Spirit's temple, which is His sanctuary for the fugitive from sin and so a hospital for the real, not-fictitious sinner, a place of mercy, above all spiritual mercy for those who fail in earthly life and have made ruin of themselves and others.

It should (though it does not) go without saying that the temple of the Spirit, which knows Christ as the Samaritan who has been neighbor to us wounded by sin and left to die on the road, attends promptly and without hesitation to the visibly wounded man who lays literally before the eyes, left to die on the road. Yet such, like the wounded man of Jesus's parable, are innocents. If compassion for these is (or should be) easy for those who have received mercy, how much greater the burden of love to be born when the wounds are self-inflicted sin that also injures and offends me! Just so the temple of the Spirit is not a fortress for perfected saints, but a hospital for forgiven sinners where forbearance is therapy in learning love.

Who believes? Who *can* believe in this concrete and visible way in the church as the Spirit's temple? The church believes as *creatura Verbi,* as recipient of the gospel concerning Christ, the good Samaritan of our

111

souls, and thus it is constituted as the Spirit's temple, the inn to which the broken are brought for healing funded by the savior. Ever before it is the agent of Christ, the risen Lord's earthly body in the world, or the people of God sighing on the way to be gathered and landed safe on Jordan's shore, the church is the communion or *koinonia* or exchange or circulation formed not *from the agreement and common intentions of believers with each other... [but] rather, the church is formed by the message of Christ proclaimed in the power of the Holy Spirit. When the Spirit awakens faith in the gospel as the good news of redemption, this message is confessed in common by people who thereby come together as sharers in it and its saving power.* The distinction is of enormous practical import. As already brought to the Spirit's temple, "the mother that begets and bears every Christian through the Word of God,"[5] members do not self-activate to form a religious club of the like-minded (the sure recipe for disunity and fragmentation) but have been passively borne, like a child from the mother's womb or the wounded man on the Samaritan's donkey, to be nursed and nurtured in the Spirit's hospital of mercy, assembled as patients treated alike by the severe mercy and merciful therapy of the love of God in Christ the crucified.

The image of temple can and indeed must be supplemented by these further images of hospital and maternity, for it can otherwise invite all sorts of unwarranted associations. It could easily evoke the image of a bubbling stew of enthusiasm, where each and every person gets to make up their own spirituality. In the significant passage from 1 Corinthians 6 from which this teaching on the temple of the Spirit draws, however, the context is the struggle of the Corinthian community to own one another in Christ as Christ has owned them. This struggle is framed by Paul between chapter 1's proclamation of the word of the cross that in Spirit and power has called them out of this passing age of partisanships into new fellowship and chapter 15's proclamation of the future resurrection that brings this present struggle to bear with one another in love to victorious conclusion. Paul's use midway through the epistle of the second-person plural pronoun is obscured in the English translation, which is here altered to bring out its social or ecclesial meaning: "Or don't you [all] know that your body is a temple of the Holy Spirit who is in you? Don't you

[all] know that you have the Holy Spirit from God, and you [all] don't belong to yourselves? You [all] have been bought and paid for, so honor God with your body" (1 Cor 6:19-20). The clumsy English makes it clear that the body of Christ is first of all the Spirit's temple, the gathering of those ransomed from this dying world.

The teaching in John where Jesus speaks of His body as the new site of God's dwelling with humanity in Spirit and in truth leads in the same direction. As one contemporary scholar has explained:

> The "incarnation" is John's theological concept for the true *worship* of the true God, which is an event which occurs first of all within the life of God, namely, the Son's self-offering to the Father in the power of the Spirit. The worship of the church comes to participate in this divine event, which precedes the church and comes to incorporate its worship through the gospel. In this way, it accomplishes the inclusion of the nations that the temple of Jerusalem should have achieved but did not.... The evangelist uses a verb in John 1:14 that says literally that the Logos "tabernacled" among us, evoking memories of early Israel's pristine worship in the desert wandering [see Exodus 33:7-10]. Indeed, John relocates the story of the Cleansing of the Temple from its place in the Synoptic Gospels to the beginning of Jesus' activity ([John] 2:13-22), making of this episode a heading over all that follows. Thereby the entire ensuing conflict leading up to Jesus' death and resurrection is defined theologically in 2:21: Jesus "was speaking of the temple of his body" [NRSV] that would be destroyed and then rebuilt in three days. To the Samaritan woman at Jacob's well, the Johannine Jesus declares, "You worship what you do not know; we worship what we know, for salvation is from the Jews. But the hour is coming, and is now here, when the true worshipers will worship the Father in spirit and truth, for the Father seeks such as these to worship him" (4:22-23 [NRSV]). The evangelist organizes his narrative of Jesus' activity around the scheme of three visits to Jerusalem and the temple during the major Jewish festivals; by this device he repeatedly contrasts the old from the new worship Jesus brings. It is a special emphasis of the Johannine passion narrative to make survival of the temple cult the pretext of the conspiracy to put Jesus to death—for the alleged blasphemy of Jesus in making Himself the Temple of God (11:48). Indeed the very first occurrence of the term "the Jews" (which might better be translated the "Judeans," those first-century Jews politically, economically, and religiously attached to the temple in Jerusalem) in 1:19 ("This is the testimony given by John when the Jews sent priests and Levites from Jerusalem to ask him,

'Who are you?'" [NRSV]) likewise indicates that what is at issue between Jesus and "the Jews" in the Fourth Gospel is the supersession, not of the Jewish people, but of the temple in Jerusalem by the new community in Jesus whom the Father gathers in the Spirit for true worship. Immediately following this exchange in 1:19, not by accident, comes the true witness from Israel, John the Baptist (notorious, like the Essenes, for his scathing critique of the temple establishment in Jerusalem). He introduces Jesus to the Gospel's readers: "[Look! The] Lamb of God who takes away the sin of the world" (1:29). Jesus is the One who will fulfill Israel's hope for atonement and communion with God, superseding the temple in Jerusalem.[6]

Incorporated into Jesus as the Spirit's new temple, believers learn to love one another as Jesus has loved them. This Johannine and Pauline therapy comes first. No one can actively be a "little Christ," as Luther put it, to another who is not first a patient of the Spirit, brought to this temple to be remade into Christ's member by the therapy of learning the mercy of the Lamb who takes away the sin of the world.

The church ever comes into being *suffering* the Spirit's baptism into Christ's death, then, before it arises to its newness of life as Christ's body in mission to the nations and within them. The church is always first of all this shared suffering in Christ, where the sharing or solidarity is what makes the suffering merciful and the bearing of one another's burden joyful. The recipient church, which thus believes as it receives, and knows that it believes not in its own power but by the gracious work of the Spirit, is such that every believer is not only personally linked to Christ by baptism but also through Christ is linked in turn to every other one so linked personally to Christ.

Just so, it is not as if regenerate individuals activate themselves and so come together for fellowship and service and thus form for themselves a religious club, but rather that Christ by the Spirit calls and gathers to Himself a fellowship of the dissimilar in order patiently to teach love for one another. *This precludes regarding church merely or even primarily as a human social reality, for God assembles the church so it may share in the triune divine life.* And this participation may be said to begin with the Spirit's will and work as just described in building a temple not made with hands or made of stones, not a temple to appease or manipulate God with crude or sublime sacrifices but a temple as hospitality, where God's dwelling begins to wipe every tear from human eyes and make all things new. The temple of the Spirit consists first of all in this fundamental and enduring receptivity that makes the palpable first experience of the ecclesia in the world hospitality—most precisely, the Spirit's hospital for sinners on the way to healing and health, righteousness and life.

Precisely as such, however, the patient church arises as agent of Christ in the world: "Your sins are forgiven. Stand up and walk!" (from Mark 2:1-12). Knowledge of the mandate to be Christ to others as Christ has been to each (Rom 15:7) and all leads to agreement *on the priority of the task of evangelizing the world, on the central significance of proclaiming and celebrating the grace of God in worship, and on the commandment to serve humanity as a whole.* The body of Christ is exercised in *the missionary imperative, asserting that the gospel message of grace and reconciliation compels those who have heard and accepted it to bring it to those who have not heard it or who have still no proper opportunity to accept it.* The jaded Christians of Euro-America today are often bewildered by the sheer joy of new Christians in the Two/Thirds world for whom evangelization is the delightful priority of sharing the good that has been unexpectedly received—a salutary bewilderment for those who need the joy of salvation restored to them!

It would today be a serious mistake at least in the Euro-American context, however, to think of evangelization as proselytizing nonbelievers or other-believers as if restoration of the cultural success of Christianity as a religion were the goal or that ambassadors of Christ were entitled to bring these others in by hook or by crook. Because of the historical record this mistake must be clearly identified and repudiated, if a vigorous renewal of mission—that is, of the agency of the body of Christ in the world—is to be gained in the coming ecumenical church. On the other hand, it is clearly to be recognized and appreciated that it was precisely the missionaries who first realized this mistake and ignited the ecumenical movement to correct it. Ecumenism and mission belong together as temple of the Spirit in which we own one another as members of the same body of Christ sent into the world, not conformed to the world, but transformed.

Factionalism, denominationalism, un-self-critical confessionalist partisan-ship—these all are secularizations of church that turn the proclamation of the good news in Christ into proselytizing for the success of our camp or tribe at the expense of others.

The key to the right use of the image of the church as body of Christ is that it is and remains subject to its Head. Members are thus to have the same mind in them as was in Christ Jesus, who did not covet divine status but emptied Himself in service of love (Phil 2). The call to repentance and faith in Jesus's name sounds forth from His servant body at work in the world, such that the call is holistic and comprehensive, *championing human dignity and inviolable human rights, providing generous aid in situations of special distress, and working on projects directed toward promoting long-term solutions to overcome misery . . . in all areas of social life—in politics, education and nurture, health, science, culture and the mass media.* The new agency in Christ proclaims His gospel in word *and deed,* as befits the body of this Head. The new agency in Christ consists of the mission to the nations and the vocations of the baptized within them.[7]

The gospel call issued in the world by the church as the body of Christ thus essentially anticipates the goal of God, the coming of the beloved community, as something greater than the present and visible church, as Paul teaches in the great meditation of Romans 9–11. For God has consigned all to sin *in order to have mercy on all.* All Israel, then, will be saved, the inclusive people of God. Already from Abraham onward God's people were summoned to blessing by which all the nations of the earth would be blessed (Gen 12:1-3). In continuity with and fulfillment of this Israel of God *the church's ultimate goal is consummation in God's kingdom, for God will create an eternal reign of righteousness, peace and love. Through grace, God has chosen and established the church **in** this age as temple of the Spirit **for** this age* as body of *Christ to proclaim the gospel to all people. . . .* So *the people of God look forward to completing their pilgrimage in a great gathering of all the redeemed on the final day.* This final unification of the sign, the inclusive people of God from all nations, and the thing signified, the consummation of all things, we yet await in the patiency of faith and activity of love. The church is triumphant not by the exclusion of any but by inclusion of many.

So this complex reality is the church. The Spirit calls and gathers together to unite with the Son, who incorporates into His mission until every contra-divine power is defeated and God becomes all things to everyone. When and if we see and hold together these three dimensions of church as recipient of merciful grace, as agent of Christ in the world, and as anticipation of universal fulfillment, we overcome much of what has actually divided Christians by parochial, one-sided, and distorted emphases on one dimension only artificially poised against the others of what is a complex, dynamic, and living whole—a living work still in progress. But because to believe in the church at all is to believe its participation in the missions of the Son and Spirit to redeem the creation and bring it to fulfillment, despite all failure there remains to the believer in God to whom all things are possible *a certainty of Christian hope that the church, established by Christ and led by his Spirit, will always remain in the truth, fulfilling its mission to humanity for the sake of the gospel.* This certainty of hope believes that the gates of hell cannot prevail. Concretely, it believes that the church cannot so fall away that *what is essential for salvation* is lost *because it is and will be preserved by the Holy Spirit.* This assured perseverance of the saints, however, is and must be constantly tested by the whole church under the authorizing word of the gospel, as attested by the apostles. Such mutual testing is what now occupies Luther and Leo in their purgatorial conversations.

CONVERSATION

Leo pondered Luther's christological argument against docetism, as also his own concern about a kind of practical docetism in Luther's denial that the bread changed into the body of Christ could or should be adored as Christ Himself for us. He was both intrigued as a humanist thinker but also repelled as a pope by the high claims implied by Luther for the work of theology within the life of the church. Certainly we are to test the spirits, as it is written in 1 John 4:1-3, to see whether they are of God.

117

But who said this was the job of academic theologians, themselves more often than not oracles of the Zeitgeist? Leo certainly understood the ecclesiastical need to distinguish Christian truth from heresy. But that was his own calling and office as chief pastor of the church. What troubled him was that Luther seemed to assume that testing was in the competence of any baptized Christian, even though de facto the specialty of the learned doctors in the university. This concern was coupled with the implication that *innovation* in doctrine, as opposed to *development* from the seeds deposited with the apostles, might be expected, indeed, at the Spirit's own prodding. Why else the need to test spirits at all if not because new forms of putatively Spirit-inspired speech occur?

Just so, Leo worried, despite all that had thus far been said and even agreed upon, who had ever heard of justification by faith *alone*? The worry now caused all of Leo's suspicions to return and multiply. Had not Paul himself already in Romans corrected his one-sided polemical statements against the law and its works in Galatians? And had not James, the brother of the Lord, who would surely know His thinking, further clarified the difficult language of Paul about "faith without works" as dead faith that even devils possess? Peter, too, in his second letter, noted the obscurity of Paul's formulations. The holistic reading of the apostolic deposit led the early Catholic Church to the doctrine that one is justified by faith operative in love and its works. The scholastic theologians had made this catholic doctrine precise in saying that love is the form of faith, without which faith is shapeless and inchoate, unable to advance the believer to righteousness. Was all this consistent development of doctrine now to be rejected? Was Luther right in his divisive innovation, *sola fide*, and the entire catholic tradition wrong? Even if he and Luther had achieved clarity and consensus on justification after extended purgatorial deliberation and debate, nonetheless, had he, Pope Leo X, not been right on the earth to warn the faithful against Luther's one-sided innovation in doctrine that inevitably and dangerously implied to the simple the falsity of the previous tradition or the blasphemy of justification by the good luck of being born into a Christian culture with its nominal faith? When all was said and done, wasn't Luther just stubborn and proud to insist on *sola fide*?

And wasn't his pride deserving of the punishment he now experienced in the hereafter as his paradoxical doctrine had been deserving of rejection on earth?

So the question of authority in the church, first raised by the German papists, came roaring back in Leo's mind.

"Dr. Luther," Leo started afresh, "how can you have so much confidence in the theologians, especially the university theologians? Where in Scripture or tradition do you read that God gave the governance of the church over to theologians? Does not the church need a properly ecclesiastical form of governance—of bishops, not academics? What kind of church would that be, subject to every new academic fad, handed over to charismatic intellectuals and their schemes undisciplined by the yoke of ordination with sacred vows and pastoral conscience, duties, and practices? You call yourself a critic of scholastic theology, but I do not see in the end that, despite your change over to a humanist method, you are all that different from scholastic partisanships, academic egos, and the cultivation of rival schools."

"You realized," the pope continued, "that there were no academic theologians for the first thousand years, not until the universities were founded four centuries ago. Even then, at first, the task was to consolidate Christian truth from its manifold forms and defend it as a unified system of belief against the attacks of Jews and Muslims and philosophers. Now I agree with you: before long, the scholastic solution became the problem of rival schools. That is why the need of a referee arose to impose limits on academic speculation for the sake of the unity of the church. This palpable need corresponded with increasing clarity about the magisterium invested in the pope and the college of bishops."

"You are indeed a good scholar," Leo concluded, "and I have learned from you in our conversations. You have convinced me step-by-step of the propriety of your reading of the Apostle Paul on the righteousness of God in Christ for faith. But that academic achievement and insight is a contribution, and only a contribution, to the doctrinal theology of the Catholic Church, which is the product of a living tradition, the stewardship of which is invested in Peter and his successors."

Luther was taken back by Leo's new intervention to the moment when he stood before the emperor and the diet and pronounced the fateful words that would doom him to the stake and the flames. Faced with the demand to recant categorically all the books he had published, he had demanded in turn to be shown specifically where he had erred on the basis of the word of God and logical reasoning: "Unless I am convinced by the testimony of the Scriptures or by clear reason (for I do not trust either in the pope or in councils alone, since it is well known that they have often erred and contradicted themselves), I am bound by the Scriptures I have quoted and my conscience is captive to the Word of God. I cannot and will not retract anything, since it is neither safe nor right to go against conscience. May God help me. Amen."[8] Luther now recalled that his *legal* demand in these *legal* proceedings was not to be vindicated without question, but quite to the contrary: to be shown as an erring brother just what his error was by way of reasoning the evidence from clear Scripture. Otherwise he would be forced to capitulate in servile fashion on threat of losing temporal life and eternal salvation. This demand of conscience to be clearly shown his error on the basis of the word of God was to be met, he realized now, not in law or in life but in divine purgatory. Yet, as the temporal demand for rational answers to rational questions then was sincere, he was at peace even with this unexpected twist of fate.

"Dear Leo," Luther replied, "I see that you, too, know a thing or two about the historicity of theology. You ask why I have confidence in academic theology, when I have been such a critic of scholasticism. The problem is not scholarship but scholars who do not understand the special subjectivity of the theologian, whether she is a theologian of glory or a theologian of the cross, a philosopher trying to uncover the cause of causes from the beginning, or a theologian who hopes against hope for the promised future of God. I am focusing on *who* believes and *why* they believe, for not all belief is the same even if the ostensible belief is in the same things: 'Not everybody who says to me, "Lord, Lord!" will get into the kingdom of heaven' (Matt 7:21). One can believe true things falsely and even false things truly. In matters of the Spirit, these much suppressed

120

questions in scholasticism about the subject of theological knowledge, must come out of the closet and into the light of day."

"But that is not to diminish academic theology," Luther immediately added. "I understand the academic work of scholarship in general, and of theology, too, so far as it is an academic discipline to be rooted in the mandate of creation that we read in Genesis 1:26-28, 'Be fertile and multiply; fill the earth and master it' (v. 28). This blessing and task are addressed to all humanity made in the image of God for likeness to God. Science through scholarship thus has this high dignity and holy calling to aid humanity in its rule of the earth in partnership with the Lord of the universe. What we have learned in the scholarly struggle for truth and clarity under the light of nature, therefore, holds also in the field lighted by grace, as we theologians see with double vision though we see one and the same world as others. For surely you are right that Christian theology is also an ecclesial discipline, and just here the question of theological subjectivity becomes crucial, so that what is seen by scholarship in the light of nature will now be illumined by the light of grace. You will recall—if, that is, you actually read it—that this is how I explained my understanding of the divine calling of theology in the life of the church and how, in all that I have written that provoked the controversies beginning with the scandal of the indulgences and preachers abusing your name and office, I have only and simply done my called duty as a theologian of both university and church."

"No," Leo mumbled, "I don't recall that I read anything like that."

"I testified," Luther continued, "that I desire to say or maintain absolutely nothing except, first of all, what is in the Holy Scriptures and can be maintained from them; and then what is in and from the writings of the church fathers and is accepted by the Roman church and preserved in the canons and papal decrees." So Luther had identified the *sources* of Christian theology.

"But," he continued, "if any proposition cannot be proved or disproved from them I shall simply maintain it, for the sake of debate, on the basis of the judgment of reason and experience." So Luther also acknowledged the *method* of theology, along with the presupposition, which so disturbed Leo, that there are things that cannot be established or developed solely from the deposit of faith yet must be debated and judged by reason and experience in order to speak newly that same deposit. Although Luther qualified this disturbing claim by denying that he would violate the judgment of his superiors in such matters, he immediately qualified this qualification on the grounds of "Christian liberty." By this he wanted to protect conscience. He would not be forced apart from his own conscientious judgment either to accept or to refute human opinions in theology. The *task* of theology, he rather affirmed, is to "examine everything carefully and hang on to what is good," as written in 1 Thessalonians 5:21. Thus, he drew that rather surprising conclusion, given his reputation as stubborn, "I believe that it is made sufficiently clear that I can err, but also that I shall not be declared a heretic for that reason."[9]

"But, Luther!" Leo could hardly contain himself. "You *were* given ample opportunity to be dissuaded and shown your error. You call it 'conscience,' but in fact you *were* merely *obstinate*. Distinguished emissaries from Cardinal Cajetan to Karl von Miltitz listened, counseled, pleaded, cajoled, and wrangled to avert catastrophe. You know, then, that this is how we define a heretic, not, as you rightly said, as someone who errs, but rather as one who, despite all efforts to the contrary, clings to his error after having been shown it."

"This I deny," Luther retorted. "I was never *shown* my error in the matters that concerned me, about the true treasure of the church as the gospel of the grace and glory of God, which ought to have premier place in the church, clearly exhibited and freely offered. This was my announced concern, not the child's play of indulgences, from which your own papists quickly retreated when all the world began to see through the fraud. Instead, I was told that I was in error simply and solely because in the process of debate, my teaching corrected the exaggeration of papal powers made in the sale of indulgences. Read my works for yourself!" Luther forgot momentarily that books and libraries were not available in purgatory. "You will see that I was myself a devoted papist—an *enthusiastic* one![10] I wanted to save your office from the discredit that abusive merchandizing of the things of God was bringing upon it."

"What kind of 'enthusiastic papist' is it who diminishes the office of the keys given to Peter and his successors?" Leo barked.

"This kind!" Luther rejoined. "One who views the keys as given for opening the gates of heaven rather than closing them! The office of pope, if it is divinely given, cannot be in essence anything other than the pastoral office that feeds the sheep and tends the lambs and leads them safely home. The pastoral office has authority to care for souls, to convince and convict consciences in relation to God and divine judgment, to guide precious sheep to green pastures and still waters. What does the Lord say to Peter in John 21? 'Feed my lambs! Take care of my sheep!' (vv. 15-16). The pastoral office should provide precisely what I had demanded before the diet, when I asked to be treated as an erring brother who needed in his conscience to be shown rationally how he erred from the Scriptures he owned and shared with others as word of God. This pastoral office, my lord, tells how *you* failed *me*. You failed to be pastor to me. You did not chase after the lost sheep but feared for the ninety-nine. If you are indeed a pope, you were no pope to me!"

"No, no!" said the pope with a new note of anguish in his voice. "If I was no pope to you, you were no son to me!"

"Did you not read? I wrote a treatise—intentionally free from all polemics with the German papists—to set forth a clear and mature statement of my doctrine, which was under suspicion on account of their outrageous caricatures. It was titled the *Freedom of the Christian*, and it clearly and patiently explained the paradox of the Christian's double existence and vision, how by faith in God through Christ he is raised up a free lord on the earth subject to none, save Christ his Lord, and at the same time humbled, as Christ humbled Himself, in love toward all others. No one reading this treatise could with justice accuse me of robbing love in order to exaggerate faith on behalf of a kind of cheap grace that forgives without conversion, repentance, or change of life. What I taught in explaining the paradox of Christian existence this way was the *freedom to love*. And furthermore, to make this doctrine even clearer to the whole world, I prefaced it with an open letter at your address. Did you not read?"

Leo was silent.

"I will tell you, then, what I there wrote," Luther said, and he spoke the words exactly as they appeared in the letter:

> I freely vow that I have, to my knowledge, spoken only good and honorable words concerning you, Leo, whenever I have thought of you.... I have called you a Daniel in Babylon; and everyone who reads what I have written knows how zealously I have defended your innocence.... Indeed, your reputation and the fame of your blameless life, celebrated as they are throughout the world by the writings of many great men, are too well known and too honorable to be assailed by anyone.... Therefore, most excellent Leo, I beg you to give me a hearing after I have vindicated myself by this letter.... I would wish you all good things eternally.[11]

Now you hear from my own lips here face-to-face that I was wishing you all good things eternally. But what about then? Did you not read? Did you not see the truth? Why did you rush to judgment against me?"

The impassioned Luther was telling the truth, for the most part. The open letter to Leo was his final testimony for the record, before he would draw the dire conclusion that the pope who condemned the doctrine of Paul and Augustine in Luther could only be antichrist who takes his throne in the temple of God. So before the world he wrote to Leo "as a lamb in the midst of wolves,"[12] alluding to the plot in the curia to poison him, which became known in 1518. The judgment Luther pronounced was not yet on the person of Leo or even the papacy as such. Instead, Luther aimed his wrath at the Vatican bureaucracy. "The Roman Curia is already lost, for God's wrath has relentlessly fallen upon it. It detests church councils, it fears reformation, it cannot allay its own corruption."[13] In face of such an enemy, he repeatedly made the personal appeal as to a father in faith, "Moved by affection for you, I have always been sorry, most excellent Leo, that you were made pope in these times, for you are worthy of being pope in better days."[14] Or again, "O most unhappy Leo, you are sitting on a most dangerous throne. I am telling you the truth because I wish you well."[15] "Now you see, my Father Leo, how and why I have so violently attacked that pestilential see. So far have I been raving against your person that I even hoped to gain your favor and save you if I should make a strong and stinging assault upon that prison, that veritable hell of yours,"[16] the Curia, the Vatican bureaucracy. "Therefore, my Father Leo, do not listen to those sirens who pretend that you are no mere man but a demigod so that you may command and require whatever you wish."[17] It is enough, he concluded, for holy father to be the servant of the servants of God as servant of a present Lord, the Good Shepherd.

The one fault that Luther acknowledged in the open letter to Leo, and indeed acknowledged again before the emperor and the diet, was that in his polemical writings he had "stormed with such great fury merely for the purpose of overwhelming my unequal opponents by the volume and violence of words no less than intellect."[18] But this concession of fault was too late by far. The damage done by Luther's excessive indulgence in verbal violence was done and could not now be undone. Bridges had been burned. Leo, consequently, never read the treatise or the open letter prefacing it because it never crossed those burnt bridges to reach him. Yet one pearl could still be extracted from the open letter to Leo. In arguing for the pastoral nature of the office and authority of the pope, and setting this understanding against the imperial pretensions of the papal court, Luther commented sharply that the apostles properly "called themselves servants of the present Christ and not vicars of an absent Christ."[19]

Here in a nutshell again is the christological critique Luther had made at the conclusion of the deliberations with Leo over Eucharist and sacrifice. The resurrection of the crucified Jesus cannot mean His removal from earth to some heaven above, such that he now delegates a kind of juridical power to Peter and his successors in His absence. He may indeed fittingly entrust the keys that open heaven to Peter and his successors, for the resurrection of the crucified Jesus means that He is and can be present as the friend of sinners who He was in His earthly mission. The keys are the word and sacraments, as the Spirit works through them as through means where and when it pleases God. Because this Head is present in and to His body this way, the church can know the mind of the Lord and test for fidelity to it. So it is fittingly the Peter who cried, "Depart from me, Lord, for I am sinful man," *this* Peter who was restored by grace won at the cross after shameful denial, the confessing Peter who fittingly administers to others the same merciful grace of the risen Lord, crucified for him, and now present through him.

Leo, still shaken at the thought that he had failed to be pastor to Luther, replied weakly, "No, it cannot be. Such failure would be lethal error."

"It was lethal!" Luther snapped, reminding Leo of the obvious.

"I have sinned, that is clear. But I meant 'lethal' officially, not personally, that is, such failure would be a lethal refutation of the promise of Jesus that the Spirit will lead the church to all truth. It is not possible, therefore, that we could have erred so grievously in office. It cannot be."

"Why do you say that?" an exasperated Luther rejoined. "It is not at all so. In the community of forgiven sinners, cannot the saving truth to which the Spirit leads and in which we are truly preserved in faith, be such that even grievous sins, apparently lethal to the church's credibility, are forgiven? Forgiven if only we have the grace to say the truth about them so that our sin is known and shown to displease us? That *is* the saving truth of the gospel! Can we not agree that *the church does not have the truth at its disposal? It has the promise that it will remain in the truth if it allows itself constantly to be called back to it.*"

"Yes, I concede this," Leo said without hesitation.

"This church shall be and abide forever," Luther continued. "I believe that there is on earth a little holy flock or community of pure saints under one head, Christ. It is called together by the Holy Spirit in one faith, mind, and understanding. It possesses a variety of gifts, yet is united in love without sect or schism. Of this community I also am a part and member, a participant and co-partner in all the blessings it possesses."[20]

"To be sure," Leo replied. "But you are changing the subject. The question is not about salvation by grace but about authority to teach the truth of salvation by grace. How is this authority to teach the truth—including this truth about God's truth that we do not possess as if to dispose of it as we please—ever to be used or exercised?"

"Am I changing the subject? How else is the truth of a *miracle*—for *that action of God* is what repentance and the forgiveness of sins *are*— to be taught except by believing and so doing? Why not teach then by acknowledging the sinful rush to judgment and overturning my unjust

126

excommunication? Even if I erred (which in substance I do not concede), I was not and am not a heretic for erring and for conscientiously protesting that my alleged error has not been dealt with pastorally. But you have certainly erred in failing to be a pastor to me, if in fact I was in error. Indeed, all the more so if I was not in error!"

"It is irrevocable. What I have written, I have written. It cannot be undone. What good now in any event would a posthumous vindication of Luther do?"

"Only in hell are things irrevocable." Luther paused. "But we are in purgatory where what was done can be overcome with new deeds. It is true that what was done cannot as such be undone. But what was done can be overcome by making new history, by doing new miraculous things such as repentance and forgiveness. As the miraculous church of forgiven sinners, we are not bound to our sinful past and the proof of this—the only demonstration of this available to us now—is in believing and so doing repentance and forgiveness."

"If we admit to error like this," Leo puffed, "we might as well all become Protestants. It would be the *end* of the Catholic Church!"

"No" Luther retorted adamantly, "it would be the *reform* of the Catholic Church. It would mean that doctrine or proclamation that intends to bind consciences—true doctrine and authentic proclamation can do no less than bind conscience, just as I confessed before the emperor and the diet—must be *open to examination by the whole people of God. Believers have the right and duty to consult Scripture in order to test whether the proclamation offered to them accords with the gospel.* This extended process of theological deliberation does not abolish teaching authority but rather broadens the magisterium to include the *consensus fidelium.* Thus *all members of the church, according to their respective callings, take part in the responsibility of teaching.* As our Lord said, "My sheep hear my voice and they will not harken to the voice of a stranger."

The pope's face reddened. "Luther, listen! This sounds good, but practically it is a recipe for chaos in the church. Didn't you notice what a can of worms you opened in your short life with this idea of permitting everyone the right of private interpretation? If I am to believe you and not confuse you with other so-called reformers who openly repudiated catholic doctrine, doesn't the fault for this confusion lie at your door when you maintain 'no fixed rules,'[21] or teaching office for that matter, in the interpretation of Scripture?"

Luther demurred. "Since justifying faith is awakened and the Church is gathered only by the pure preaching of the Gospel and the evangelical celebration of the sacraments, communion and its preservation require agreement in the right understanding of the Gospel. We have sought such agreement primarily by means of explicit confessional consensus documents adopted by congregations and churches. In such a confessional communion the communion of churches also finds visible expression."[22]

"This supposed agreement on doctrine is a communion in the mind only! It is not a visible reality in the world," Leo retorted. "Show me a church that actually corresponds to this confessional communion and I will deal with it! Otherwise you are the Platonist and docetist!"

"The Church as a human fellowship is by nature a fellowship in solidarity," Luther replied. "This fellowship impels a common participation in material and spiritual needs and in material and spiritual resources, and it presupposes fellowship in the confession of the faith and includes fellowship in the office of word and sacraments, in common actions and decisions that take on an authoritative character. It is by nature a committed fellowship. Commitment is not optional; it impels the community toward common life and action."

"Well said," Leo replied, "but since it is nothing but ideas the committed fellowship you allege falls to pieces when one local church allies with its native people and nation against another people and nation. The Church *in* Germany then becomes the church *of* Germany and Christ's church becomes the people's church."

"We need a communion of communions to express the fact that fellowship in Christ is simultaneously universal and particular," Luther acknowledged. "Repeatedly, historical challenges arise in the face of which the relation to the universal Church is decisive for the particular church and its decisions. Conversely, the needs of a particular church demand action and decision from the universal fellowship. At the same time, this church of churches is not a coerced and prescribed uniformity. It realizes itself in a variety of forms, all looking beyond what is to what will be. It lives from its communion with the Lord, who is Lord and Savior of all creation and serves him as sign and instrument for the salvation of the world."[23]

"Again, well said," Leo nodded. "But where is the institution that can deliver these things? Otherwise they are just words and ideas that fly in the face of the countervailing and entrenched tendencies toward the local over the universal."

"Fellowship in the Eucharist is unthinkable without fellowship in the faith that takes on a normative form through councils and synods. Those who do not accept the faith in this normative, doctrinal form exclude themselves from the *communion*," Luther replied. "The needed institution is a true and perpetual council of churches.

"I do not deny that what you say is a Catholic form of thinking,[24] even if you imagine a church of churches without an institution within it embodying the universal church," Leo answered. "The event in which [Jesus's] Lordship and his messianic role burst forth in full light, his cross culminating in his resurrection, is the event in which he takes upon himself the human condition in its deepest level of poverty. He is made the Lord of the kingdom in the supreme moment of his communion with the rejected, the despondent, the hated, the excluded, the scorned, the ridiculed, the martyrs. The kingdom is a kingdom of the 'poor,' not only because they are heirs of it, but also because it is by identifying himself with their fate that Jesus has overcome it.[25] This is the universal of the church that requires its own institutional form and representation. Indeed, this notion of salvation as sharing implies—although many have been reluctant to say this openly—that Christ assumed not just unfallen but *fallen* human nature. So the institution may be populated with fallen beings, but that does not disqualify it. I, Leo, I dare say, am proof of that, as I am here with you in this place of final preparation. Look, Christ lived out his life on earth under the conditions of the fall. He is not himself a sinful person, but in his solidarity with fallen man he accepts to the full the consequences of Adam's sin. He accepts to the full not only the physical consequences, such as weariness, bodily pain, and eventually the separation of body and soul in death, but also the moral consequences, the loneliness, the alienation, the inward conflict. It may seem a bold thing to ascribe all this to the living God, but a consistent doctrine of the incarnation requires nothing less.[26] And a consistent doctrine of the incarnation also requires a papacy that upholds this gospel truth when local churches deviate from it."

"I teach only what I have first learned," Luther pointed out. "Jesus's sacrificial act on the cross is his giving of himself to the Father for us and inseparably his giving of himself to us in obedience to the Father. What he gives is therefore communion: our communion with him, and just so our communion with the Father and with one another.[27] The institution corresponding to this a church of churches."

"But precisely in that case," Leo jumped, "are faith in Christ and identification with the church community distinguishable spiritual acts? Or is the Christ who is both the ground and object of faith the *totus Christus*, the embodied person whose body is the church?"[28]

"It would seem to follow."

"Can we have Christ at all apart from the church, granting that the church is a church of churches?"

"It would seem to follow."

"Does such a church as you describe exist among your followers?"

Luther was silent.

"Here is a fact. Scripture is a dead letter. It does not speak for itself. Scripture is always interpreted Scripture. It can be interpreted by the church as the church's book, or it will be interpreted by others for other purposes! That it be interpreted according to the analogy of faith is the special task and duty of the magisterium. Why, you yourself are an expert at selecting texts for emphasis to the neglect of other texts that speak against your presumably authoritative interpretation, which slap and dash you gussy up as 'Scripture interpreting Scripture.' In fact, you work with an unwarranted canon within the canon—something other than the faith once delivered to the saints and entrusted to Peter and his successors for safeguarding."

"Now," Leo continued, "I don't just get to make things up any more than you do. This teaching ministry is *a painstaking quest for the truth, in which the faithful, bishops, and theologians participate.* But we are lost to abject Protestant confusion and the chaos of reader response silliness unless we hold that *the bishops, in communion with the bishop of Rome, are authentic teachers of the faith by virtue of their episcopal ordination as successors in the presiding ministry of a local church.* This authentic teaching authority is *not contrary to the gratuity of salvation given in justification. The teaching ministry as such serves the communication of doctrinal truth, not the mediation of forgiveness of sins and justifying grace.*"

"Ah," Luther sighed, momentarily feeling defeat. "*Here, deeply rooted convictions meet and oppose each other.*" Truth of God and salvation in Christ—are these two different orders or one? Does the former guarantee the latter? Or is the former an implication of the latter?

For all their progress in purgatory, Leo and Martin had come to an impasse. Roman authoritarianism or Protestant chaos—what a miserable choice lay before them, exposed in plain sight for both to see! Lethal Christian contradictions between essentialist Catholics and existentialist Lutherans.[29] "Who will deliver me from this body of death?" the Apostle signed! For the body of Christ divided in this "deeply rooted" way literally cannot act, being internally at cross purposes. Like cancer cells that will not die, but live on parasitically destroying the host, these deeply rooted convictions of the wounded body only rip the more and further tear.

SIGN OR GUARANTEE?

A fter a long winter in purgatory, Leo reopened the deliberation with
a poignant statement of his deeply rooted conviction.

"It is springtime, Luther. Our Lent must end and Easter come."

"Let it be," Luther agreed.

"The ministry of Peter and his successors," Leo began, "is malleable
in form and subject to development in conformity with the gospel, as
we have come to understand it together, as the Spirit leads us to discover
*forms in which this universal ministry may accomplish a service of love recog-
nized by all concerned.* I acknowledge," Leo continued, "that *the Catholic
Church's conviction that in the ministry of the bishop of Rome she has preserved the visible sign and guarantor of unity constitutes a difficulty for most
other Christians, whose memory is marked by certain painful recollections*—as
you have rehearsed to me with no little force, brother Martin, in our last
round. *To the extent that we are responsible for these, [we] ask forgiveness.*"

Luther was touched. He felt that this was coming. But he was also
perplexed. "Yes, yes," he almost gushed. "I forgive! But what does this
reconciliation mean?"

"Could it not mean that the real but imperfect communion existing
between us…leads us to a patient and fraternal dialogue on this subject
of the ministry of Peter, a dialogue in which, leaving useless controversies
behind, we could listen to one another, keeping before us only the will of

133

Christ for his church and allowing ourselves to be deeply moved by his prayer 'that they may all be one.'"[1]

"I would leap, dear Leo, I would kiss your feet and carry you on your throne on this way forward. Yet I am abashed. I am almost fearful to say it. I don't want to jinx this fresh start."

"Say what is troubling you, my son."

"I can accept the papacy as a 'sign of unity' if it is clearly understood as the universal pastoral office of oversight, for the ministry of oversight is certainly evangelical and found in the Scriptures. But how could I ever accept that this ministry, which you identify with the office of the bishop of Rome to which you ascribe Peter's apostolic ministry—*this* ministry that excommunicated me and had me and many others sent to the flames—is a 'guarantor of unity'? Sign yes, guarantee no. Have not historical record and fact amply shown this presumptuous guarantor inflicted disunity, not least by coercing its own jurisdiction? Is this what you ask me to overlook when you ask that we leave 'useless controversies behind'? Then it will be, I fear, a phony reconciliation not founded on this most pertinent truth of Scripture, 'If we say we have no sin we deceive ourselves and the truth is not in us. But if we confess our sins, God who is faithful and just, will forgive our sins and cleanse us from all unrighteousness.'"

"But Dr. Luther," Leo calmly replied, "did you not yourself teach me that we are to unify the sign and the thing signified?"

"No, I taught that this unification is the work of the free and sovereign Spirit, who blows as He will, whom we can only believe. We pray this unification and in faith we expect it; we act with fear and trembling to anticipate it. But in so doing we may err. We do not possess it as something to be taken for granted and so come to use at our own whim. We are—both—at the mercy of the Spirit!"

"In this place," Leo dryly remarked, "that has become painfully obvious," glancing down and not wishing at the moment to make eye contact with his stubborn interlocutor. "Let me start afresh this new start. You said that you agree on the necessity of the ministry of oversight."

"Yes, of course," Luther said. "In fact, we were forced to it ourselves almost immediately when we saw how miserable the state of the church was when we were sent on a visitation. Visitation, you know, *is* the ministry of oversight! Out of this experience, I wrote my catechisms to inculcate the faith, equip the ministers, and empower the laity—all in all to assist the development of a mutual ministry of oversight. I say, though, we were *forced* to undertake this ministry of oversight ourselves because the regularly ordained bishops would not do it—warlords in chasubles, one and all of them! Money-hungry aristocrats in robes! They cared not a lick for the perishing souls in their dioceses, only for the endowments and income streams! These pseudo-bishops refused to ordain our priests and then accused our priests of lacking canonical orders. But I say that bishops who persecute the gospel are not bishops. Bishops who exploit souls rather than feed them are not bishops."

"No, brother Martin. You don't understand ontology very well, do you? They may be bad bishops. They may even be, as you say, traitors like Judas. But only a disciple can be a traitor. Only a bishop can be a bad bishop. Abuse cannot erase their calling and sacred ordination."

"It is not that I don't understand your ontology but rather that I don't much care for any ontology that has not yet been revised by Christian eschatology to show the proleptic character of being, the church, too, and the ordained ministry within it."

"What do you mean by that?" Leo asked, as if for the first time considering a new and unfamiliar thought.

"By 'proleptic' I mean an eschatological ontology, a metaphysics of anticipation as opposed to the protological ontology of the philosophers, a metaphysics of persistence.[2] Life is not godliness but the process of becoming godly, not health but getting well, not being but becoming, not rest but exercise. We are not now what we shall be, but we are on the way. The process is not yet finished, but it is actively going on. This is not the goal, but it is the right road. At present, everything does not gleam and sparkle, but everything is being cleansed.[3] What is real is not what persists in spite of time, but what in time anticipates our final future."

"So I ask you, Leo, if bishops or pastors can sin in this way, as you admit, and abuse, even betray their office, what good is it to say that episcopacy properly ordained in the succession of the laying on of hands reaching back to the apostles *guarantees* unity? That the laying on of hands in succession is a sign of the intention of God and the church to minister in keeping with the apostles is true, but trivial. We, too, lay hands on our new pastors and by doing so intend to signal the same apostolic fidelity and succession in doctrine, which is what really matters. But this rite guarantees nothing. On the contrary, teaching that it guarantees obscures what otherwise would be plain for all to see in the crimes and abuses of the clergy. So what good is it?"

"It is good for sending bad bishops to purgatory, as you have seen in *me*, dear Luther! It is good for holding the clergy *doubly* accountable! Why, our Dante thought it was good for sending simoniacs to the eighth circle of hell!"

"I suppose it is good for that," Luther grumbled, who had learned before his death of the deal between Leo and Albrecht of Brandenburg that stood behind Tetzel's indulgence campaign. Simoniacs were those who bought or sold ecclesiastical offices, named after the Simon in the book of Acts who tried to bribe Peter to acquire the Holy Spirit. But Luther had not actually read the *Inferno*. So he changed the subject: "But the question I am asking is how it is that it guarantees the thing signified, our union through Christ with one another as temple of the Spirit and body of Christ and people of God?"

"Let me turn a little of your historical critical scholarship back on you, Martin. You have too much of this medieval image of the warrior pope or warlord bishop stuck in your head. The office of bishop in the local town, city, or territory, as the case may have been, was the form of ecclesiastic ministry that emerged in the course of the second Christian century in taking up and passing on the unique ministry of the apostles against the profound challenge from Gnosticism, which taught a secret succession from Jesus not publically knowable. There were not two or three different Christian denominations on Main Street, you know, but all the believers of a locality were united under the Eucharistic presidency of one overseer, the bishop. We know this already from the letters of Ignatius of Antioch, who campaigned for unity with the bishop as the sole leader of the catholic Christians in any given place and in sharp distinction from them who despised the public assembly in preference for their private conventicles. He did so to oppose the heresy of docetism, as you yourself noted and emphasized in our previous discussion."

"I have been thinking that over ever since," Leo paused to make sure that Luther was attending to his history lesson. "As you know, docetism denied that Jesus Christ had come in the flesh because it despised everything flesh and saw salvation as deliverance from all that is visible and tangible and public: the visible church, the visible Eucharist, the visible love and charity of believers, the visible presidency of the one bishop. As Ignatius in chains, after being arrested and being transported to Rome to die for the Lord as His martyr, refuted the docetists with the singular rebuke of all the martyrs who confess the Lord Jesus in their own flesh in defiance of the death threats of this world: 'If Jesus only seemed to die, then I only will seem to be torn to pieces by the lions!' Carrying through this down-to-earth realism, Ignatius thus warned against spiritualistic docetists:

> Mark those who hold strange doctrine concerning the grace of Jesus Christ which came to us, how that they are contrary to the mind of God. They have no care for love, none for the widow, none for the orphan, none for the afflicted, none for the prisoner, nor the hungry or thirsty. They abstain from the eucharist and prayer, because they do not allow that the eucharist is the flesh of our Savior Jesus Christ, which flesh suffered for our sins, and which the Father in his goodness raised up.[4]

"Now, dear Luther, all this down-to-earth, in-the-flesh ecclesiology is bound up with christological antidocetism, up to including episcopacy, which public office of presidency developed against the docetist threat as the normative form of that public ministry *to* the Word and sacraments of Christ, so that *from* the Word and sacraments of Christ the body fed and nourished presents itself for free and joyful service of love in the real world of flesh and blood. This ministry of human service Ignatius assigned to the diaconate emblemized the vocation of all the baptized people of God."

"Leo, Ignatius I know and Ignatius I honor. Must it here be recalled who also died as a martyr?"

"No," Leo again turned away from Martin, abashed. "No need to say so." He paused and then continued. "You are right to mention this. Now

I am the one caught in his own net. If we are not docetists, we also cannot just lay aside the Luther affair as a useless controversy now passé."

"My personal reputation matters little to me," Luther responded, unwilling to press the point further. "What does matter is the confession of faith that I made, also in my death, and that others have made with me. This public confession demands recognition by you as a catholic possibility and indeed as a Christian contention for the truth of the gospel that speaks also to you and those in communion with you."

"What are you saying, Luther? You already know that I welcome you and all those who follow you to return to Mother Church!"

"I thought we had seen together earlier," Luther reminded, "that according to my confession of faith I never departed from the Catholic Church. Speaking of 'return' will never reconcile us."

"What, then, will?"

"Call the bluff!" Luther explained. "My own suspicion is that many of those who claim to be my followers share in my antipapist polemics, which they have broadened into a general anti-Catholicism, but are far from my confession of faith. And it is my confession of faith that demands and deserves your Christian recognition. Don't you see that if you allowed this confession of faith its status as a Catholic possibility, the real question would transpose and become something far from 'useless'? Now the question becomes whether or not there really is a church that corresponds to this confession of faith. That means a body that could act according to its conviction of faith to actualize with you a new unity of the church!"

"Let me point out, brother Luther, that you are agreeing with me about the need for conscience-binding doctrine as well as the capacity of the church to define it."

"Of course, why would there be any doubt about this?"

"I suppose because your followers regularly opposed the gospel as the word of God to church doctrine as the word of man and absolutely forbid their identification. To be clear, what I am affirming is *the conviction that the episcopal and papal magisterium can articulate the truth of the gospel in doctrinal affirmations that express or interpret divine revelation [that] the faithful are obliged to accept with a religiously based assent.*"[5]

"They are followers who have not listened to me very carefully then," Luther replied, for the moment stifling the fire within him at the clericalism of Leo's statement. "This abstract dialectic of the word of God and the word of man is not how I talk about church doctrine. The Spirit, I say, gives us formulas of language to which we are bound in conscience, even when they appear innovative. So it was at Nicea with the *homoousios* and so, I dare say, also in the *sola fide*. You wonder how can I say this, when I also reject human speculation and philosophical intrusions on theology. But the answer is not difficult. If it is true, as I teach, that faith justifies because faith is the gift of the Spirit to receive the gift of the Word incarnate, then our hearing and confessing of the word of God is no less divine speech than the speech of God spoken to us in Christ. In doctrine we preach the gospel back to God and the world, saying, 'This is what I have heard and believed and thus confess.' Such confession of faith is quite distinguishable from speculations stemming from human wisdom because it is recognizably the Spirit's response to the word of God spoken. When I make my confession of faith, then, I am freely binding my conscience to assert and maintain in the confidence of the Spirit, 'Thus I have heard and understood the word of the Lord!' So anyone who in my name claims that *any teaching claiming to be binding must be met with a reservation regarding its binding nature* misunderstands me. When teaching does not articulate the gospel, I am conscience bound to protest, not merely reserve judgment. And when any teaching does articulate the gospel, I am conscience bound to attest it."

"Well said, dear Luther," Leo concurred. It struck him as right and very reassuring, since for apostolic succession, succession in faith is the essential aspect and further, that even if preserving correct doctrine is not the task of the ordained ministry alone, it is still its specific task to teach and proclaim the gospel publically. Why else would ordinands make vows before God and the church, if not publically to bind their consciences in just this way to the church's public confession of faith? Indeed, the capacity of the body of Christ to act in the world in tested and testable conformity to its Head consists in such conscientious commitment to the confession of faith.

139

So Leo pushed the point: "A church as the body of Christ is capable of acting. It has agency. It can do things. That is what the claim for the episcopacy as the fullness of ministry intends to claim, in which the priests or presbyters and deacons participate in any given locality. What is at stake here in episcopacy is not a literal claim to an historical succession traceable back to the apostles in the rite of the laying on of hands. That notion and its ritual enactment can only be a sign of the intention to teach in continuity with the apostolate; and I am persuaded now that this rite is hardly different from the Lutheran pastor's pledge to teach in continuity with the book of the apostles, the New Testament. But what *is* at stake is the Pauline idea of 1 Corinthians that there is only in any given locality one Church of Christ; this is signed by the presidency of one bishop. And through this bishop the local churches are related to one another in the translocal college of bishops. And among these bishops, the Spirit led the churches to recognize the Petrine function taking residence in Rome."

"All this," Luther said, mellowing, "I could accept as pious opinion, but to dogmatize it on pain of salvation is an act of tyranny. You know that the primacy of Roman jurisdiction is expressly rejected in the canons of the Council of Nicea; so the Greeks have never accepted it. And the scandals that have attended it in recent centuries make the claim so grossly implausible that pious opinion can scarcely survive an honest reading of the history books."

"The papacy is the Spirit's work in progress," the chastened but still papal Leo replied. "Could you not realize that your pointed critique might actually aid and assist in my summons to seek together *the forms in which this ministry may accomplish a service of love recognized by all concerned*? Do you see that this open and collaborative discussion of 'forms' portends the reform of the papacy to a form that is transparently a service of love? Wouldn't that count as success in your own eyes?"

"What else have we to do here in purgatory," Luther winked, "but engage in such thought experiments?"

"Very well, then!"

"Alright, let me ask this question then," Luther pressed. "If the interdependence of assembly and ordained ministry is typical of the structure

140

of the church at the local, regional, and national level, then why should such an interdependence not also be found at the universal level? If so, the entire church would take responsibility for magisterium and the danger, not to mention historically justified fear of papal tyranny would be much abated. I am in this way open for the possibility of the ministry of Peter as a visible sign of the church as a whole, on the condition that this ministry is subordinate to the primacy of the gospel in a structure where that relationship can be tested theologically by the interdependency of local and universal church."

"No," said Leo abruptly. "The universal church is both ontologically and epistemically prior to local churches, for Jesus Christ is the same yesterday, today, and forever. As head, He is ontologically and epistemically prior to human faith in Him, which faith is always some local appropriation, inculturation, and contextual synthesis. A pope with a universal ministry to the unity of the church would be pointless if this ontological priority were not the case. The church is founded on the rock of Peter's confession. The confession of Jesus Christ the Son of God is the universal truth of revelation that unifies the local churches. Local churches inevitably tailor the truth of the gospel to their contexts, and in time these local adaptions make the local churches so strange to one another that they cannot recognize one another as one and the same Catholic Church. Fragmentation is the result. The necessity of the ministry of the universal truth is to keep local churches in communion on the basis of the revealed truth of Jesus Christ."

"So," Luther groaned, "you have taken up my *solus Christus* and turned it against me! But look, what are you saying but that in the end you presume to think of yourself as the vicar of an absent Lord, not the servant of a present one? You are wrong to take this work of Christ alone upon yourself because that is unfaith that would try to secure what can only be freely given and received in faith. Because this is so, we cannot be better 'ruled and preserved than if we all live under one head, Christ, and all the bishops—equal according to office (although they may be unequal in gifts)—keep diligently together in unity of teaching, faith, sacraments, prayers, and works of love.'[6] An honorary first among equals, perhaps, at best; but not the supposed embodiment of the Head on earth and vicar of an absent Lord!"

"Look at us here, Luther!" Leo cried. "He is absent! He leaves us to work it out in His absence!"

"No, He is with us even in the belly of the whale, even as once for all He descended to the dead. He is not absent but hidden!"

So near but so far! Thus the deliberation in purgatory had advanced but now stalled, *raising questions that have no promise of imminent resolution.*

ON THE WAY TO CHRISTIAN PERFECTION

A long, sullen silence filled the isolated corner of purgatory where Martin and Leo dwelt, broken only when a new voice sounded in their midst. "I have read of you both, and, Martin, I have studied your works. In fact, I was already a priest of the Church of England when I heard your very words read aloud. The date was May 24th, 1738..."

"The year of our Lord, 1738?" interjected Leo, aghast at how much earthly time had lapsed in the interim.

"Indeed, that was already many years ago," the newcomer continued. "I was ready to quit the ministry, so cold was my heart and barren my soul. But at an evening prayer meeting in Aldersgate, someone read, Martin, the following words from your *Preface to Romans*. I have never forgotten them because they changed my life and ministry." So the newcomer recited Luther's words from memory:

> Faith is a divine work in us. It changes us and makes us to be born anew of God (John 1); it kills the old Adam and makes altogether different men, in heart and spirit and mind and powers, and it brings with it the Holy Spirit. Oh, it is a living, busy, active, mighty thing, this faith; and so it is impossible for it not to do good works incessantly. It does not ask whether there are good works to do, but before the question rises, it has already done them, and is always doing them. Faith is a living, daring confidence

in God's grace, so sure and certain that a man would stake his life on it a thousand times. This confidence in God's grace and knowledge of it makes men glad and bold and happy in dealing with God and all His creatures; and this is the work of the Holy Spirit in faith. Hence a man is ready and glad, without compulsion, to do good to everyone, to serve everyone, to suffer everything, in love and praise to God, who has shown him this grace; and thus it is impossible to separate works from faith, quite as impossible as to separate heat and light.[1]

"That's it!" Leo cried. "I couldn't have said it better myself! Martin, why haven't you spoken to me in these words, if in fact they are yours?"

"They are mine," Luther acknowledged, unwilling to explain how in the course of time he founds his own words imperfect in the same way that he came to regard Augustine's words on justification imperfect for not making sharply the abstract point that faith alone justifies, that is, considered apart from its impossible separation from works of love. The tangled web was not worth untangling at this late date.

"It was," the newcomer continued, "about 8:45 p.m. While these precious words of Luther sounded describing the change that God works in the heart through faith in Christ, I felt my heart strangely warmed. I felt I did trust in Christ, Christ alone for salvation; and an assurance was given to me that He had taken away my sins, even mine, and saved me from the law of sin and death."

A stunned silence followed before Luther approached the newcomer. "I am pleased and gratified to meet you, sir," Luther said. "This is my roommate, Pope Leo X, but we address each other by first names here."

"And who are you and why are you here?" Leo queried.

"My name is John Wesley; I am an Englishman and, as I said, a priest of the Church of England. The 'warming of my heart' transpired at the words Martin wrote concerning the change in human desire and affection that attends faith in Christ. Becoming convinced of this was the decisive reorientation of my life in ministry. I became consumed with the very passion of faith he described to live a busy, active, mighty life of love, preaching to the poor and ignorant of England and the New World."

144

As Martin and Leo pondered the information, Leo ventured: "I had heard of the New World. Charles of Spain intended to claim it for the cross of Christ."

"Yes, Leo, so he did, but not in a manner of which I approve. It is by the persuasion of preaching, not the force of steel, that faith that changes us and makes us born anew to God ought to be spread."

"Yes," Leo nodded, "I have come to see that in these years. You see, Luther and I have been put here together as our purgatory and cannot leave until we leave together to sit together at the Great and Heavenly Banquet."

"So I was informed just before I joined you," Wesley replied. "I have been sent here to join you."

"Why?" Leo asked. "What wrong have you done?"

"Nothing so particular," Wesley said matter-of-factly. "It is just that I have not yet reached that blessed state of Christian perfection that fits one to see God face-to-face."

"Neither have we!" Luther chimed in. "It has been almost three centuries, it seems, and we are still working on it! Sin-ruled by Christ in us is not yet sinlessness."

"The more progress we make, it sometimes seems, the greater the distance between us appears to be," Leo sighed.

"I was told," Wesley said sympathetically, "that somehow we each have something that the other needs so that only together can we find our way forward. Neither can I advance to the Heavenly Banquet apart from the two of you. You, too, are my purgatory."

"Do we prefer this interminable purgatory to our eternal destiny?" Leo asked.

"Are we trapped in logics of self-justification forever?" Luther queried.

"Even about our doctrines of justification?" Wesley retorted.

"Pray God that it not be so," Leo almost shouted. He was feeling hungrier than ever.

"Then let me venture this," Wesley said, summoning up all his pulpit excellences. "So profoundly good in being is God's creation, Leo, that you have wanted to speak of redemption as the grace-assisted act of the human creature as modeled in the Virgin's word, 'Let it be unto me according to your word.' It is as if the image of God was but slightly tarnished in the fall. So profoundly warped in being is God's creation, Martin, that you have wanted to speak of redemption as the grace of a new creation arising from death in Christ to His resurrection. It is as if the image of God was changed in the fall to an image of the devil. Polemical exaggerations aside, you are both right!"

"Another Protestant paradox-preacher," Leo thought to himself.

"But only in such a way that both truths," John continued, "can be seen to complement rather than contradict each other. For the truth is that we were created in the image of God in order to acquire likeness to God. In the fall, Adam surely lost the likeness, but as only a human being can be a sinner, so only one made in the image of God can fail to be like God. But Jesus Christ is the likeness of God restored to us, and in Him our humanity is redeemed. One needs the giant sweep of the entire biblical canon to see how these two truths complement each other. One has to realize that redemption in Christ is not God's second thought, but His first thought in the creation of the world. *Felix culpa*! Oh, happy fault of Adam![2] The new creation is a deed of redemption that was integral to God's creative purpose from the origin."

Wesley was introducing reflections to Luther and Leo on the impasse to which Reformation and counter-Reformation theologies had come in the intervening centuries. As he made clear in his self-introduction to Luther, *he felt deeply indebted to the biblical teaching on justification as it was understood by Luther and the other reformers.* But as a member of the Church of England, he had *also always embraced elements of the doctrine of justification [that] belong to the Catholic tradition of the early church both East and West. This gave his own doctrine of justification its distinctive profile.* This reconfiguration amounted to a reframing of the doctrine of justification beyond the narrow, even exclusive focus on the human role in justification, which framework tacitly held the sixteenth-century interlocutors in its grip. This focus imposed a false binary, making either human passivity or human activity decisive in justification. Wesley thus particularly welcomed news of the consensus on justification, which Leo and Luther now reported to him at length. Their consensus seemed to him to have in fact transcended the inherited framework that parsed the question of justification purely on the plane of anthropology.

"What you were just saying seems to approach what we have converged upon in this purgatorial interim," Leo concluded his report to John.

Luther added immediately, "Yes, we have agreed *that justification is the work of the triune God. The Father sent his Son into the world to save sinners. The foundation and presupposition of justification is the incarnation, death, and resurrection of Christ. Justification thus means that Christ himself is our righteousness, in which we share through the Holy Spirit in accord with the will of the Father. Together we confess: By grace alone, in faith in Christ's saving work and not because of any merit on our part, we are accepted by God and receive the Holy Spirit, who renews our hearts while equipping and calling us to good works.*"

"I very much appreciate this statement," Wesley responded earnestly, "and I am *especially grateful for the trinitarian approach by which God's work in salvation is explained* in it. What one must see in a more adequately trinitarian framing of the doctrine of justification is a distinction but not a separation of the redemptive works of the Son and the Spirit. The Son gives Himself to us as a ransom from sin, and the Spirit gives Himself to us that we can receive the Son, unite with Him, grow in Him, and at last fully be conformed to Him."

Wesley was indeed gratified to associate himself with the convergence between Luther and Leo. The deep connection between forgiveness of sins and making righteous, between justification and sanctification, has always been crucial for the Methodist understanding of the biblical doctrine of justification. John Wesley saw in salvation a twofold action of God's grace: "By justification we are saved from the guilt of sin and restored to the favor of God; by sanctification we are saved from the power and root of sin, restored to the image of God."[3] The redemptive acceptance into communion with God and the creative renewal of our lives are entirely the work of God's grace. Acceptance and renewal are sequenced. We must be first—always first!—accepted by God's grace as the favor and good pleasure of our heavenly Father in order that we be renewed by just this acceptance and grace rather than by meritorious deeds of our own piety or practice. But as the Son and the Spirit are distinct persons in the life of the one God they are equally inseparable in the one God. And so also are their works.

"You know," Luther began as he slowly gathered his thoughts, "divine faith as the Spirit's work is what I was teaching from the beginning. If we are indeed justified by faith as the Spirit's work and gift in us, then the separation of justification and sanctification is not only false to Christian experience but also theologically incoherent. The unity of justification and sanctification is evident in the very passage from the *Preface to Romans* that John cited earlier. It was only later on in a polemical atmosphere and under constant duress that we felt compelled to introduce the abstract clarification that God's first imputes righteousness and subsequently sanctifies. Admittedly, people took this abstraction for concrete reality and created a dualism. You know, as a result of this awful misunderstanding, I became angry at my congregation in Wittenberg at the end for taking the great gift of Christian liberty and turning it into the license of a pigpen—so angry that I was ready to die and be done with them![4] How they cheapened the costly grace of God! How they despised the Holy Spirit—it would have served them right to be returned to the harsh discipline of papal tyranny!"

In his anger at the recollection of cheap-grace Lutheranism, Luther forgot momentarily that he himself was being disciplined by an indefinite sentence of life together with a papal tyrant.

"I see it this way," Wesley responded. "'Faith working through love' (Gal 5:6) is seen as the root of all good that results from the lives of those who believe in Jesus Christ. Works of piety and works of mercy are fruits of the Spirit in the lives of those who follow Jesus. Such works also help the believers live their lives in communion with God and to be 'God's coworkers' (1 Cor 3:9) in the field of God's mission and in ministry to the poor and to those who need the love of God most. But all such works are the work of God's grace. As I once put it in the sermon 'Working Out Our Own Salvation' (Phil 2:12): 'God works, therefore you can work. God works, therefore you must work.'[5] God's agency and human agency are not competitive, except when in unrepentant sinfulness we want to be

God and do not want God to be God! Then the Lord knocks us off our high horse as first he did to Paul the apostle on the road to Damascus. But in the same moment, the Lord bestows the Spirit of Christ to open our blinded eyes. The Spirit of Christ bestows, in turn, the mind of Christ and thus the power to be little Christs to our neighbors, Luther, as I believe you characteristically put it."

"So I preached, again and again, to no avail in my own Wittenberg congregations!"

"What I learned from the fallout of the schism," Wesley continued, "was something taught by one of your later followers, Philip Jacob Spener by name. He lamented the high and fancy preaching in the cities and towns, flattering the princes and defending true doctrine against all deviants but ignoring the common people in their ignorance and dire need. 'Numerous are those,' he wrote in his little book, *Pious Desires*, 'who do not recognize the ruin of Joseph [Amos 6:6] in many areas. They think that the church is in a most blessed condition as long as we are not hard pressed by opponents of a false religion and enjoy outward peace. They do not see the dangerous wounds all around.'⁶ So he spoke of the clergy. When he turned his attention to the laity, he observed that 'when one looks at the everyday life even of those among us who are called Lutherans (but who do not deserve this name, for they do not understand the dear Luther's teaching about living faith), does one not find grave offense—indeed, such offenses are everywhere prevalent?'"⁷

"This description by Spener," Wesley continued, "fit to a tee what I saw in my time in England and America. So I learned to bring the gospel to the common people with an emphasis on the twofold nature of the gift of righteousness in Christ as deliverance from the guilt of sin and power from on high to live ever more freed of sin. I have taken to heart the Apostle's word: 'Now that you have been set free from sin and become slaves to God, you have the consequence of a holy life, and the outcome is eternal life'" (Rom 6:22).

"But surely our sanctification is still under way," Luther protested. "We have not yet arrived even though we press on."

"Am I not now joined to you here in this place? Yes," Wesley nodded, "I affirmed the possibility of Christian perfection not the fact of it, at least in my own case."

"But I remain concerned," Luther broke in, "about even this affirmation of a possibility of perfection before the Lord comes to make all things new; it is too much like the illusion I lived under as a monk. Aspiration for perfection in the Christian life brings with it all the attendant dangers of falling back under the law, obscuring, even vitiating the peace we have with God in being justified by faith alone while still afflicted by sinfulness within and without."

"And I am concerned," Wesley maintained, "about cheap grace, grace without repentance and earnest struggle to be freed from the power of sin. I am concerned about half a gospel, which leaves us ruined by sin with a happy conscience, dear Luther. I am concerned with exactly the problem you report from the end of your days in your congregation at Wittenberg. What good is it to tell the gambler, the wife-beater, the alcoholic 'your sins are forgiven' even though you remain trapped in these sinful and destructive patterns? Our Lord said, 'Your sins are forgiven. Therefore, arise and walk!'"

Leo, listening attentively, had learned a thing or two about ecumenical dialogue in these centuries of purgatory. "Perhaps you are talking past each other. John, explain to us exactly what you mean by Christian 'perfection.'"

"I actually developed the doctrine of 'Christian perfection' or 'entire sanctification' (cf. 1 Thess 5:23), which I consider to be at the heart of my teaching. Let me explain. First, 'entire sanctification' or 'Christian perfection' is nothing else than 'loving God with all your heart and all your soul and with all your mind' and 'your neighbor as yourself' (cf. Matt 22:37-39; 1 John 2:5). Second, it is not the absolute perfection that belongs to God alone; and it 'does not imply an exemption either from ignorance, or mistake, or infirmities, or temptations.' Third, even if our whole being is filled with the love of God that has been poured out into our hearts through the Holy Spirit (Rom 5:5), this will always remain God's gift and the work of God's grace and never our human merit or achievement. Fourth, the hope of conquering sin should never lead us to deny or disregard the danger of backsliding and being caught by the power of sin. Fifth, those who are justified and sanctified by God's grace will struggle with temptation and sin during their whole lives. But in this struggle they are strengthened by the promise of the gospel that in Christ God has broken the power of sin."

"It strikes me," Leo reflected, "that with these qualifications the dynamic idea of Christian existence as growth in righteousness on the basis of the gift of righteousness in Christ, as you have explained it to me, dear Luther, is well articulated. It is not a state of rest that you describe by perfection, but labor."

Luther did not directly respond but rather asked, "Do the perfect who yet labor still need daily to pray, 'Forgive us our trespasses'?"

"If in reality one loves God above all and all creatures in and under God," Wesley replied, "there would be nothing to forgive. You have to agree with that, don't you?"

"Yes, that would be perfection! When we are in heaven! But we struggle on the earth, and even now this struggle is not ended! It is two steps forward, one step back. And the steps back are sins! And sinners are not yet perfected."

"Ah, yes," Wesley sighed, recalling that he, too, was in purgatory. "Perfection," he continued, "As to *the word*, it is scriptural. Therefore neither you nor I can in conscience object against it, unless we would send the Holy Ghost to school and teach him to speak who made the tongue. By that word I *mean* (as I have said again and again) 'so loving God and our neighbour as to rejoice evermore, pray without ceasing, and in everything give thanks.' He that experiences this is scripturally perfect. And if you do not yet, you may experience it. You surely will, if you follow hard after it, for the Scripture cannot be broken. What, then, does their arguing prove who object against 'perfection'? Absolute and infallible perfection? I never contended for it. Sinless perfection? Neither do I contend *for this*, seeing the term is not scriptural. A perfection that fulfils the whole law, and so needs not the merits of Christ? I acknowledge none such—I do now, and always did, protest against it. 'But is there no sin in those that are "perfect"?' I believe not, but be that as it may, they feel none, no temper

151

but pure love while they rejoice, pray and give thanks continually. And whether sin is *suspended* or *extinguished*, I will not dispute; it is enough that they feel nothing but love. This you allow we should daily press after. And this is all I contend for. O may God give you to taste of it today!"[8]

"How could I not join you in that prayer?!" Luther replied. "I struggle to love still. Let me explain why I think that perfectionism, even as duly and carefully qualified as you have presented, John, is concerning. Let us not even bother with the petty self-righteousness of the 'Do not smoke, do not drink, do not dance' crowd. Sin is much more subtle a power and cunning a master than that. Sin is wanting to be God and not wanting God to be God. Sin is envy of God, as the serpent enticed, *Sicut Deus eritis*!" Luther loved the Latin of the Vulgate, which he had deeply internalized in his many years as a monk, "You shall be as God!"

"I am not thinking of such big and subtle things, Luther. I am thinking pastorally and concretely of the abject plight of the masses, just like Spener did. Look at the drunkenness! Look at the lives and families ruined by it! Look at the exploitation of the workers by the bosses who set up a bar and a brothel next to the pay table to take back the pitiful wages of the day laborers, sending them deeper and deeper into debt and misery!"

Wesley spoke at this moment prophetically, though he knew it not, about the earthly future of his movement, which would widen into the Pentecostal teaching of a second blessing of grace for those Christians living in the world but manipulated, abused, exploited, and too often crushed by sinful structures of malice and injustice. These Christians would look not only vertically for forgiveness from God above but also horizontally for power from on high to overcome the penetration of the sinful world into their own souls. At their best they would pray not only for personal power to live as disciples but also for reform in the direction of more just and less malicious forms of social life.

"Yes," Luther agreed excitedly, "bread and circuses to keep the masses under their control. On this social point about envy and greed structuring malice and injustice in this wicked world, I could not agree more," Luther said, working himself into a lather.[9] "Just so, my worry is that your perfectionism underestimates this very battle we are in and in its own way focuses again on the human creature, fragile and easily manipulated, as if it could simply transcend the conditions of bodily existence. The old evil foe has sworn to work us woe. His craft and power have no earthly equal. If in our own power we had to defeat him, we would be lost forever."

"But we are redeemed," Leo exclaimed. "We are redeemed from sin by Christ. We are redeemed from the guilt of sin and, as brother Wesley rightly affirms, also from the power of sin! We can anticipate the resurrection. We can live already now as new creatures."

"By faith, not yet by sight! Has Christ finished his work of redemption?" Luther rejoined. "Is not the last power to be destroyed death? That apostolic reservation means that death remains in power, even over us who have been justified, who still must await in hope against hope that transformation of the cosmos, which the Apostle calls the redemption of our bodies and the revelation of the glorious liberty of the children of God."

"Yes," Wesley interjected, "I affirm that our bodies are both the object of redemption and the site of sanctification. Our bodies are the place in the world bought with a price. We are to glorify God in our bodies! They are to be the temple of the Holy Spirit. So teaches the same Apostle."

"Paul is speaking here of the body of Christ, of which we are individually members," Leo corrected. "My worry is somewhat different than Luther's. It is that your idea of perfection is too individualistic. The body that is perfect is the body of us all in Christ, the church. The church, taken as a social form, is the manifestation of the reign of God, the beloved community of God in the world, the anticipation of perfection."

"Well, yes and no," Luther replied. "In Christ, we are redeemed and united, yet our individual bodies are still bound up with Adam. The body is the site of the struggle of the Spirit against the flesh, not yet the victory. That is why we cry, 'Who shall deliver us from this body of death?!' That is why we wait for the revelation of the glorious liberty of the children of God who will freely, joyfully, spontaneously love God above all and all creatures in and under God. So the church is righteous in hope but sinful in fact, and this shameful fact makes its perfection to be hidden under the manifest sins of its daughters and sons, indeed of its institutional life in the world."

153

"Yes, I see," Wesley said. "You affirm Christian perfection both individually and socially but regard its consummation as something Christ has yet to achieve for us, that comes only with His manifest victory at the transformation of the common body of the cosmos."

"Precisely," Luther responded. "If we think it already possible as a present state of being, perfectionism nurtures illusions about the struggle of Christian life. We are organically bound by our bodies to the structures of malice and injustice in which we live, and move, and have our being. The food I buy, the wood I burn, the clothes I wear, the job I have, the protection of law and order I receive, the entertainments I enjoy—in short, all that makes me an inalienable member of the common body descended from Adam does not disappear when I am joined to the body of Christ. If I forget this dual membership, if not citizenship, for a moment, how easily I can delude myself as a born-again slaveholder or a born-again capitalist or a born-again male chauvinist or whatever. Truly such sinners have been born again! Do you hear what I am saying? Such sinners as are also we! Truly such sinners can become partly just in life. But perfection? We do not—indeed we cannot—know all the dimensions and entanglements of sinfulness, let alone free ourselves from them. In life I am ever learning about this, and even as I break free I am more and more being taught to pray as I struggle forward step-by-step to righteousness, 'Forgive us our trespasses as we forgive those who trespass against us.' In this prayer, I must leave final deliverance from evil to One wiser and more just than myself who will remake me whole and pure on the day of the resurrection."

Leo was rapt at this culminating interchange between Wesley and Luther, since he found himself assenting to both arguments but unable to see how they hung together as complements rather than contradictions.

"Where then is the peace and joy of the Christian life in this picture of an eternally conflicted being that you draw, Luther, as if it were the Christian being described in Romans 7?"

"Peace and joy consist in the forgiveness of sins. For where there is forgiveness, there is also life and salvation. In this life," Luther quoted his blessed Augustine, "our righteousness consists for the most part in the forgiveness of sins. We become only partly righteousness in fact. In fact, that is why we all are still here and still together, is it not?"

"Undoubtedly, if God has put us together in this purgatory." Wesley paused. "Perhaps true perfection and advancement toward it consist in learning in deed, not only in words, to forgive as we have been forgiven." Wesley then added, "*It is our deep hope that in the near future we shall also be able to enter into closer relationship with Lutherans and with the Roman Catholic Church in accordance with this declaration of our common understanding of the doctrine of justification.*"

"But we are not there yet," Leo nodded.

"No," Luther agreed. "Not yet, if repentance, as you both rightly maintain, consists not only in the easy words, 'I am sorry,' but also, as John the Baptizer thundered, in the fruits that befit contrition. Yes, that means making repairs joyfully, like the tax collector Zacchaeus did. Joyfully to repair paradoxically arises from *true* sorrow, not over the punishment but rather over the sin. It is the lifelong labor of baptism into Christ's death, a wrenching renunciation of a self that has ever wanted even in the name of the good what was not good, a Spirit-wrought reconstruction of a new self, then, that wants the good that God wants. Not yet, if forgiveness, as we have come to see, consists in God's own good: actively abandoning the right to avenge the wrong and restoring the offender to a place of honor— as we all hold that Christ has done for us but not yet wholly in us."

"Yes," Wesley said softly, "we are not there yet."

"Indeed," Leo echoed even more softly, "we are not there yet."

THE MAN BEHIND THE SCREEN—AND YOU!

"Pay no attention to that man behind the screen!" So the great and mighty Oz thundered at Dorothy and her friends when at last they had arrived in the Emerald City, only to be exposed by the little dog Toto. This "omniscient narrator" (as he is called in literary criticism), however, will drop the veil and be his own Toto. This is the one who has just taken the reader on a journey into purgatorial suffering that has led to an anticlimactic denouement, that is, Luther and Leo, joined by Wesley, still indefinitely confined together to purgatorial quarters. How will they ever emerge linked arm and arm to enjoy the Great and Heavenly Banquet?

Now here is the peeling back of the curtain. The extended metaphor of the journey means that Christian inability to forgive in deed, not only in words,[1] keeps us in this purgatory of our ecumenical winter, and such unwillingness is true sinfulness. Repentance in deed entails repair. Leo should in deed *joyfully* revoke the excommunication of Luther as a heretic.[2] Luther should in deed *joyfully* revoke the demonization of the papacy and return, at least, to the *status quo ante* of the temporal authority of the bishop of Rome. And Wesley ought *joyfully* to facilitate this reconciliation. With the narrator's issuing thus of his plain verdict, however, he is revealed as in fact less than omniscient. With that verdict, he is in fact only passing on the baton to you, dear reader. Dear reader! How is the tale to be finished? He leaves it in your hands!

Of course, the tale could also be filled out in all sorts of other ways. We could put Luther in purgatory with the Jews he so sinfully defamed or likewise with the peasants whose cause he knew and himself had liberated from pious scruples that kept them silent about their oppression. We could put Leo in purgatory with the native peoples of the New World who were conquered and converted in his name or with the dissident Christians tortured and martyred by the Inquisition and the counter-Reformation or again with the Muslims against whom he summoned up Holy Crusade. And we could have had these two joined not only by John Wesley to point a way forward but also by many others who since have lived in dismay at, and so worked to overcome, the schism of the Western church. Such works of theological imagination are now bequeathed to you, dear reader, to write not only in words but also in deeds the new chapters on the way to the Great and Heavenly Banquet at which all—but *only together*—will feast. *Bon voyage!*

NOTES

PREFACE

1. See the very interesting book of Don Thorsen, *Calvin vs. Wesley: Bringing Belief in Line with Practice* (Nashville, TN: Abingdon Press, 2013), which provides background for the portrait of Wesley in chapter 9 of this work.

2. Jaroslav Pelikan, *The Riddle of Roman Catholicism* (New York: Abingdon Press, 1959), 212.

3. Walter M. Abbott, S. J., ed., *The Documents of Vatican II* (New York: Herder & Herder American Press, 1966).

4. Paul Tillich, *The Protestant Era*, trans. James Luther Adams, abridged ed. (Chicago: University of Chicago Press, 1966).

5. Pelikan, *The Riddle of Roman Catholicism*, 46. Seeking to overcome this deficit on the ground level are the recent contributions of Mickey L. Mattox and Gregg Roeber, *Changing Churches* (Grand Rapids, MI: Eerdmans, 2011); and Piotr J. Malysz and Derek R. Nelson, eds., *Luther Refracted: The Reformer's Ecumenical Legacy* (Minneapolis: Fortress, 2015).

6. Timothy J. Wengert, *Martin Luther's 95 Theses with Introduction, Commentary and Study Guide* (Minneapolis: Fortress, 2015,) xiii. On this topic, see also *Martin Luther's 95 Theses*, ed. Kurt Aland (St. Louis, MO: Concordia, 1967); and Berndt Hamm, *The Early Luther: Stages in a Reformation Reorientation*, trans. Martin Lohrmann (Grand Rapids: Eerdmans, 2014), 85–109.

7. *LW,* 31:135.

8. *LW,* 31:225–27.

9. See Michael Root and James J. Buckley, eds., *Heaven, Hell, . . . and Purgatory?* (Eugene, OR: Cascade, 2015).

10. Pontifical Council for Promoting Christian Unity, accessed January 14, 2017, http://www.vatican.va/roman_curia/pontifical_councils/chrstuni/weeks -prayer-doc/rc_pc_chrstuni_doc_20160531_week-prayer-2017_en.html.

1. NOT AS EXPECTED

1. There is a basis for this fiction in historical reality. See Ludwig Pastor, *The History of the Popes*, vol. 7, ed. Ralph Francis Kerr (London: Routledge & Kegan Paul and St. Louis: Herder, 1950), 258, 267, 272, 280–81, 286, 289.

2. Ibid., 291, 328.

3. Ibid., 218, 227, 232, 235.

4. Daniel Levering Lewis, *God's Crusade: Islam and the Making of Europe, 570–1215* (New York and London: Norton, 2008).

5. For an extended analysis, see Kenneth M. Setton, "Pope Leo X and the Turkish Peril," *Proceedings of the American Philosophical Society* 113, no. 6 (December 1969): 367–424.

6. *LW*, 31:92.

7. Pastor, *The History of the Popes*, 94, 256, 278.

8. Ibid., 279.

9. Ibid., 307–8.

10. Ibid., 256.

11. Peter Brown, *The Rise of Western Christendom: Triumph and Diversity A.D. 200–1000*, 2nd ed. (Oxford: Blackwell, 2003), 433.

12. Pastor, *The History of the Popes*, 136; on Leo's reputation as a result for intrigue and equivocation, see further 99, 101, 105–7, 110, 117–18, 153, 262–63.

13. The great early theorists of secularization were of course Thomas Hobbes in England and Samuel Pufendorff in Germany. See Paul R. Hinlicky, "Irony of an Epithet: The Reversal of Luther's Enthusiasm in the Enlightenment," in *A Man of the Church: Festschrift for Ralph Del Colle*, ed. Michel Barnes and Mickey L. Mattox (Eugene, OR: Wipf and Stock, 2013), 302–15; and "The Reception

of Luther in Pietism and the Enlightenment," in *Oxford Handbook to Martin Luther*, ed. R. Kolb, I. Dingel, and L. Batka (Oxford, UK: Oxford University Press, 2013), 540–50.

14. Compare to Brad S. Gregory, *The Unintended Reformation: How a Religious Revolution Secularized Society* (Cambridge, MA: Belknap Harvard University Press, 2012).

15. Quentin Skinner, *The Foundations of Modern Political Thought*, 2 vols. (Cambridge, UK: Cambridge University Press, 1978).

16. *LW*, 31:130–31.

17. Ibid., 31:153. Cf. 125–30.

18. Ibid., 31:216.

19. "I follow the rationale, though not all the details of the Lutheran Forum Guidelines on inclusive language." Paul R. Hinlicky, "Preface," *Luther and the Beloved Community: A Path for Christian Theology after Christendom* (Grand Rapids: William B. Eerdmans, 2010), xxiv. See also "Editorial and Confessional Standards," American Lutheran Publicity Bureau, accessed February 27, 2017, http://alpb.org/editorial-and-confessional-standards/.

20. Philip Freeman, *Julius Caesar* (New York: Simon and Schuster, 2008), 66–68.

21. See Dennis Bielfeldt, Mickey Mattox, and Paul Hinlicky, *The Substance of the Faith: Luther's Doctrinal Theology for Today* (Minneapolis: Fortress, 2008); Christine Helmer, *The Trinity and Martin Luther: A Study on the Relationship between Genre, Language and the Trinity in Luther's Works* (1523–1546) (Mainz: Verlag Philipp von Zabern, 1999); Graham White, *Luther as Nominalist: A Study of the Logical Methods Used in Martin Luther's Disputations in the Light of Their Medieval Background*, Schriften der Luther-Agricola-Gesellschaft, vol. 30 (Helsinki: Luther-Agricola Society 1994).

2. A Blessed Griefwork

If memory is correct, I first heard this remarkable expression, "A Blessed Griefwork," from the lips of the late Dorothee Soelle, the German feminist theologian who was a visiting professor as Union Theological Seminary NY when I was a graduate student.

1. Scott H. Hendrix, *Luther and the Papacy: Stages in a Reformation Conflict* (Minneapolis: Fortress, 1981).

2. *LW*, 31:169.

3. Ibid., 31:155.

4. Oleg Bychov, "An Invitation to Pope Leo X" (unpublished paper).

5. *LW*, 31:171–72.

6. Ingolf U. Dalferth, *Crucified and Resurrected: Restructuring the Grammar of Christology*, trans. Jo Bennett (Grand Rapids: Baker Academic, 2015), 28–37.

7. See Luther's significant *Disputatio de divinitate et humanitate Christi* (1540) in WA 39/II, 92–121.

8. Paul R. Hinlicky, "Metaphorical Truth and the Language of Christian Theology," in *Indicative of Grace, Imperative of Freedom: Essays in Honor of Eberhard Jüngel in His 80th Year*, ed. R. David Nelson (London and New York: Bloomsbury and T & T Clark, 2014), 89–100.

9. Pastor, *The History of the Popes*, 28; Herbert M. Vaughan, *The Medici Popes* (London: Methuen, 1908), 9–13.

10. Vaughan, *The Medici Popes*, 47-61; Pastor, *The History of Popes*, 138–39.

11. Vaughan, *The Medici Popes*, 55; Pastor, *The History of the Popes*, 30.

12. Pastor, *The History of the Popes*, 33.

13. Pastor, *The History of the Popes*, 23, 26, 27; Vaughan, *The Medici Popes*, 109, 130.

14. Vaughan, *The Medici Popes*, 106.

15. Pastor, *The History of the Popes*, 34.

16. Ibid., 218; cf. 227.

17. Ibid., 235.

18. Ibid., 199.

19. Ibid., 170-75.

20. Ibid., 175.

21. Ibid., 197, 207.

22. Ibid., 184.

23. Ibid., 278–79.

24. Vaughan, *The Medici Popes*, 170–74, 182–25; Pastor, *The History of the Popes*, 166.

25. Jeremy Kruse, "Hunting, Magnificence and the Court of Leo X," *Renaissance Studies* 7, no. 2 (1993): 243–57; Pastor, *The History of the Popes*, 399.

26. Vaughan, *The Medici Popes*, 77–78.

27. Ibid., 157.

28. *LW*, 31:190.

3. MEMORY RANSACKED: LUTHER

1. "In 1549, three years after Luther's death, a German Catholic writer, Johann Cochlaeus, published his *Commentary on Luther's Actions and Writings,* a book that deeply influenced the image of Luther held by Catholics for more than two centuries. Sad to say, Cochlaeus wrote in the white heat of excited anger against Luther. By his own admission, Cochlaeus set out to make his readers feel revulsion toward Luther.... Cochlaeus had an eye especially for passages in which Luther attacked Catholic doctrines and institutions. The excerpts [from Luther's writings that Cochlaeus reprinted in his *Commentary*] were to show the readers a Luther quite reckless in polemics, clearly destructive of Church, clergy, and Sacraments. Cochlaeus depicts Luther as the cause of the violence in Germany in 1525, when the peasants revolted.... Luther, according to Cochlaeus, was not even consistent, but kept changing his views as occasion suggested.... In spite of the disorganization and carelessness [of his *Commentary*], Cochlaeus's image of the devilishly destructive Luther dominated Catholic popular understanding of Luther for centuries." Jared Wicks, S.J., *Luther and His Spiritual Legacy* (Collegeville, MN: Michael Glazier, 1984), 15–16. Likewise, erstwhile Lutheran Jaroslav Pelikan: "The prime mover [according to Roman Catholics] was the 'heresiarch' Luther. Although he had said some sensible things at the beginning, he 'steadily deteriorated' and became 'the first to break the bond of peace and unity.' . . . 'The whole business depends on the one man, namely, the author of the schism': Luther himself had become the chief issue, 'Martin the heretic, Martin the schismatic, Martin the prince of utter pride and temerity'; and he remained so also

after his death." Jaroslav Pelikan, *The Christian Tradition: A History of the Development of Doctrine, IV: Reformation of Church and Dogma (1300–1700)* (Chicago: University of Chicago Press, 1984), 246. In Eck's own words, after listing 404 such quotations from Luther and his "sons," taken out of context and patched together to form a single whole: "All the articles above noted, both those of Luther himself, as clearly a man familiar with the devil, and those of his followers who, being infatuated with his errors, have so degenerated as to become deaf to the truth, we reject and anathematize." J. M. Reu, ed., *The Augsburg Confession: A Collection of Sources,* (St. Louis: Concordia Seminary Press, 1966), 120.

2. *LW,* 31: 334–43.

3. "One cannot overestimate the importance for the traditional Catholic view of the Reformation and of the Lutheran position of the catalogs of heresies drawn chiefly from the statements by the Reformers of the first half of the 1520's, principally by Johannes Cochlaeus, Johannes Eck, Johannes Faber, and Alphonsus de Castro. According to this view, the focal point of the Lutheran doctrine and the 'source and origin of almost all other heresies' is Luther's doctrine 'that faith alone is sufficient for the salvation of everyone.' The Reformation way of speaking about faith alone justifying was interpreted as teaching that the Sacraments accomplish nothing, that good works are superfluous, and that nothing can endanger faith. This view was supported by quotations of exaggerated Reformation statements taken out of context, and often obtained second or third-hand." George W. Forell and James F. McCue, ed., *Confessing the One Faith: A Joint Commentary on the Augsburg Confession by Lutheran and Catholic Theologians* (St. Paul, MN: Augsburg, 1982), 134.

4. *LW,* 31:379–95.

5. Rüdiger Safranski, *Nietzsche: A Philosophical Biography,* trans. Shelley Frisch (New York and London: Norton, 2002), 300–303. On the specific differentiation from Luther (and Augustine!), see pp. 297–98.

6. E.g., *LW,* 31:107–14, 118–19.

7. On this problem, see Heiko Oberman, *Luther: Man between God and the Devil,* trans. E. Walliser-Schwarzbart (New Haven, CT: Yale University Press, 1989); and Mark U. Edwards Jr., *Luther's Last Battles: Politics and Polemics: 1531–46* (Ithaca, NY: Cornell University Press, 1983); see further Paul R. Hinlicky, *Luther and the Beloved Community* (Grand Rapids: Eerdmans, 2010), 379–85.

8. *LW,* 31:163.

9. Alisdair MacIntyre, *After Virtue: A Study in Moral Theory* (Notre Dame, IN: University of Notre Dame Press, 1984).

10. For this genealogy, see Paul R. Hinlicky, *Beloved Community: Critical Dogmatics after Christendom* (Grand Rapids: Eerdmans, 2015), 34–55. For most helpfully complexifying the usual trope of Luther against scholasticism, see Theodor Dieter, *Der junge Luther und Aristoteles: Eine historisch-systematische Undersuchung zum Verhältnis von Theologie und Philosophie* (Berlin & NY: Walter de Gruyter, 2001).

11. Ernst Käsemann, *Essays on New Testament Themes,* trans. W. J. Montague (London: SCM, 1971), 95–107.

12. *LW*, 31:346.

13. Adam Drozdek, *Greek Philosophers as Theologians: The Divine Arche* (Hampshire, England and Burlington, VT: Ashgate, 2007); Paul R. Hinlicky, *Divine Simplicity: Christ the Crisis of Metaphysics* (Grand Rapids: Baker Academic, 2015).

14. *LW*, 31:57.

15. St. Thomas Aquinas, *Summa contra Gentiles,* trans. Vernon J. Bourke, 5 vols. (Notre Dame and London: University of Notre Dame Press, 1975), book 1, chap. 91, para. 1–18, pp. 277–82.

16. Ibid.

17. Ibid.

18. Ibid.

19. Ibid.

20. Ibid.

21. Ibid.

22. *LW*, 34:336–37.

23. Ludwig Pastor sees this, citing Johannes Cochlaeus (he references *Meteorologia Aristotelis* s. Aij, in Otto, Johannes Cochläus, 26) already in 1512: "Humanist studies, however much they may conduce to the ornamentation of learning, are injurious to those who have no solid scientific training. Hence the levity of certain persons, to whom the name of 'poets' is erroneously given. Hence the

buffoonery and the criminally scandalous lives of some. They are the common slaves of Bacchus and Venus; not the pious priests of Phoebus and Pallas" (Pastor, *The History of Popes*, 316–17). Of course, this particular indictment might better apply (even according to Pastor's own account) to Leo rather than to Luther!

24. Hinlicky, *Beloved Community*, 97–105.

25. Saint Augustine, *Confessions*, trans. Henry Chadwick (Oxford, UK: Oxford University Press, 1998), 3.

26. Paul R. Hinlicky and Brent Adkins, *Rethinking Philosophy and Theology with Deleuze: A New Cartography* (London and New York: Bloomsbury Academic, 2013).

27. Robert Kolb and Timothy J. Wengert, eds., *The Book of Concord* (Minneapolis: Fortress, 2000), 433.

28. See further on this, Paul R. Hinlicky, *Divine Complexity: The Rise of Creedal Christianity* (Minneapolis: Fortress, 2011), 167–73.

29. Arthur H. Drevlow, "The History, Significance, and Application of Luther's Catechisms," *Concordia Journal* 5, no. 5 (September 1979): 174.

30. Luther knowledgably discusses in passing Pico della Mirandola's attempt to Platonize Aristotle in *LW*, 31:223.

31. William J. Wright, "The Influence of Renaissance Humanism and Skepticism on Martin Luther," in *The Oxford Encyclopedia of Martin Luther*, ed. Derek Nelson and Paul Hinlicky (New York: Oxford University Press, 2017). I have been further informed by two unpublished papers: Neil R. Leroux, "Pastor to the Pope: Martin Luther's Modeling of Proper Christian Service in *Epistola Lutheriana ad Leonem Decimum summum pontificem* (1520)" and Oleg Bychov, "An Invitation to Pope Leo X."

32. Martin Luther, *Luther: Lecture on Romans*, trans. Wilhelm Pauck, The Library of Christian Classics (Philadelphia: Westminster, 1961), 3.

33. "Luther's Anti-Docetism in the Disputatio de divinitate et humanitate Christi (1540)" in *Creator est creatura: Luthers Christologie als Lehre von der Idiomenkommunikation*, ed. O. Bayer and Benjamin Gleede (Berlin and New York: Walter De Gruyter, 2007), 139–85.

34. Oswald Bayer, *A Contemporary in Dissent: Johann Georg Hamann as Radical Enlightener,* trans. Roy A. Harrisville and Mark C. Mattes (Grand Rapids: Eerdmans, 2012).

35. *LW,* 31:134–35.

36. *LW,* 31:100.

37. *LW* 31:223.

38. *LW,* 31:128.

39. *LW,* 31:107.

40. On the idea of the Fatherhood of God as God surpassing God, see Hinlicky, *Beloved Community,* 691–710.

41. *LW,* 32:200.

42. Jared Wicks, S.J., *Luther and His Spiritual Legacy* (Collegeville, MN: Michael Glazier, 1984), 137.

43. David Lotz, *Ritschl and Luther: A Fresh Perspective on Albrecht Ritschl's Theology in the Light of His Luther Study* (Nashville: Abingdon Press, 1974), 133, cited from *WA* 4, part I, p. 228, line 33. Cf. *LW* 26, 129.

44. *Martin Luther's Basic Theological Writings,* ed. Timothy F. Lull (St. Paul, MN: Fortress, 1989), 251.

4. MEMORY RANSACKED: LEO

1. Pastor, *The History of the Popes,* 291, 328, 385; less charitably, Vaughan, *The Medici Popes,* 283.

2. Pastor, *The History of the Popes,* 394–95.

3. Ibid., 394. See Luther's point-by-point response in *LW,* 32:3–99.

4. Cited in Pastor, *The History of the Popes,* 356–57 from N. Paulus, *Johann Tetzel, der Ablassprediger* (Mainz, 1899), 53; see further Pastor, *The History of Popes,* 367–68. Pastor credits Luther's opponent Prierias for the clear-sighted judgement that the attack on the indulgences was only incidental and that the object of Luther's attack was the authority of the Church, 393fn.

5. Pastor, *The History of the Popes,* 357.

6. Ibid., 379.

7.Ibid.

8. *LW*, 34:334. Compare Pastor, *The History of the Popes*, 393, who argues that Luther was conspiring a religious war of bloody persecution against the Catholic Church. What is true is that Prierias raised the stakes by invoking "infallibility" (365).

9. Pastor, *The History of the Popes*, 387–88, 405–6.

10. *LW*, 34:333.

11. Pastor, *The History of the Popes*, 349. The Council of Trent surely and succinctly moved against the "pernicious abusers of the questors of alms… so that all may understand that these heavenly treasures of the Church are administered not for gain but for piety." See *Canons and Decrees of the Council of Trent*, trans. Rev. H. J. Schroeder, O.P. (St Louis and London: Herder, 1960), 142.

12. For what follows, Pastor, *The History of the Popes*, 330–33.

13. For what follows, Vaughan, *The Medici Popes*, 215–43.

14. Pastor, *The History of the Popes*, 29.

15. Ibid., 42.

16. Ibid., 316–18.

17. Lewis, *God's Crusade*, 160–83.

18. Brown, *The Rise of Western Christendom*.

19. Vaughan, *The Medici Popes*, 24.

20. Pastor, *The History of the Popes*, 5.

21. Jennifer Mara DeSilva, "Senators or Couriers: Negotiating Models for the College of Cardinals under Julius II and Leo X," *Renaissance Studies* 22, no. 2 (2008): 154–73.

22. Pastor, *The History of the Popes*, 94, 256, 278.

23. Ibid., 63, 71, 76, 103, 105, 112, 142, 163, 165, 213ff.

24. Ibid., 5.

25. Ibid., 328, 343; Vaughan, *The Medici Popes*, 182–85.

26. DeSilva, "Senators or Courtiers," 154–79.

27. Vaughan, *The Medici Popes*, 160.

28. Pastor, *The History of the Popes*, 36, 73.

29. Ibid., 166.

30. Jeremy Kruse, "Hunting, Magnificence and Court of Leo X," *Renaissance Studies* 7, no. 3 (1993): 243–57; Vaughan, *The Medici Popes*, 160–214.

31. Vaughan, *The Medici Popes*, 215–43.

32. Ibid., 157.

33. Ibid., 9–13.

34. Ibid., 55.

35. Ibid., 43.

36. Ibid., 47.

37. Ibid., 68–77.

38. Ibid., 77.

39. Ibid., 114.

40. Ibid., 106.

41. Ibid., 109, 130.

42. Ibid., 138.

43. Ibid., 170–74.

5. A Consensus on Justification

1. The infamous quotation attributed to Leo, "All ages can testify enough how profitable that fable of Christe hath bin to us and our companie," is "a spiteful and monstrous invention of a rabid or unscrupulous Reformer..." Vaughan, *The Medici Popes*, 281.

2. Words set in italics in this chapter are drawn from The Lutheran World Federation and the Roman Catholic Church, *Joint Declaration on the Doctrine of Justification*, English trans (Grand Rapids, Wm. B. Eerdmans, 2000); see http://www.vatican.va/roman_curia/pontifical_councils/chrstuni/documents /rc_pc_chrstuni_doc_31101999_cath-luth-joint-declaration_en.html.

3. In fact, Scotus, Occam, and Biel are the chief targets in Luther's early *Disputation against Scholastic Theology* (*LW*, 31:3–16). Bruce D. Marshall has shown considerable material convergence between Luther and Thomas in "Faith and Reason Reconsidered: Aquinas and Luther on Deciding What Is True" *The Thomist* 63 (1999): 1–48; and "Justification as Declaration and Deification," *International Journal of Systematic Theology* 4, no. 1 (March 2002): 3–28. But see also the incisive critique by Christine Helmer in *Theology and the End of Doctrine* (Louisville, KY: Westminster John Knox, 2014), 97–110.

4. On this internal Lutheran contradiction, see Paul R. Hinlicky, "Staying Lutheran in the Changing Church(es)," in Mattox and Roeber, *Changing Churches*, 281–314.

5. *LW*, 31:194.

6. Ibid., 31:100–101.

7. Ibid., 31:241.

8. Ibid., 31:219.

9. Ibid., 31:145.

10. Holger Sonntag, ed., *Solus Decalogus est Aeternus: Martin Luther's Complete Antinomian Theses and Disputations* (Minneapolis, MN: Lutheran Press, 2008).

6. EUCHARIST AND SACRIFICE

1. Italicized passages in this chapter are taken from 2016 Lutheran-Catholic *Declaration on the Way: Church, Ministry, and Eucharist* (Minneapolis, MN: Augsburg Fortress, 2015).

2. *LW*, 36:35, see also p. 49.

3. Ibid., 31:160.

4. Ibid., 31:94.

5. Ibid., 31:133.

6. Ibid., 31:132.

7. Ibid., 36:29.

8. Martin Brecht, *Martin Luther: His Road to Reformation 1483–1521,* trans. J. L. Schaf (Minneapolis, MN: Fortress, 1993), 382.

9. Reu, *The Augsburg Confession,* 97.

10. *LW,* 36:56.

11. Paul R. Hinlicky, *Paths Not Taken: Fates of Theology from Luther through Leibniz* (Grand Rapids: Eerdmans, 2009), 127–76.

12. Kolb and Wengert, *Book of Concord,* 477, 479

13. Dietrich Bonhoeffer, *Ethics,* trans. N. H. Smith (New York: MacMillan, 1978), 205.

14. Vaughan, *The Medici Popes,* 23–24.

15. Pastor, *The History of the Popes,* 5.

16. *LW,* 40:229–62.

17. Pastor, *The History of the Popes,* 169–70.

18. Robert W. Jenson, *Unbaptized God: The Basic Flaw in Ecumenical Theology* (Minneapolis, MN: Augsburg Fortress, 1992).

7. CHURCH AND MAGISTERIUM

1. Italicized statements in this chapter are drawn from *Declaration on the Way: Church, Ministry, and Eucharist.*

2. H. Richard Niebuhr, *The Social Sources of Denominationalism* (New York: Meridian, 1957).

3. Paul Tillich, *Systematic Theology,* 3 vols. (Chicago: University of Chicago Press, 1967), 1:8–11.

4. *LW,* 31:85.

5. Kolb and Wengert, ed., *Book of Concord,* 436.

6. Hinlicky, *Divine Complexity*, 70–71.

7. Robert Benne, *Ordinary Saints: An Introduction to Christian Life* (Minneapolis: Fortress, 2003).

8. Brecht, *Road to Reformation*, 460.

9. *LW*, 31:83.

10. Ibid., 34:328.

11. Ibid., 31:334–35.

12. Ibid., 31:336–41.

13. Ibid.

14. Ibid.

15. Ibid.

16. Ibid.

17. Ibid.

18. Ibid., 31:341.

19. Ibid., 31:342.

20. Kolb and Wengert, ed., *Book of Concord*, 419.

21. *LW*, 31:341.

22. William G. Rusch, ed., *A Commentary on "Ecumenism: The Vision of the ELCA"* (Minneapolis: Augsburg, 1990), 127.

23. Ibid., 122–23, emphasis added.

24. Susan K. Wood describes the same thinking in contemporary Roman Catholic idiom: "'Communion' integrates the two dominant images of the church at the time of the Second Vatican Council: the church as the body of Christ...and the church as the people of God....Within this integration the image of communion retrieves a biblical and patristic idea of the whole Christ, the *totus Christus*, by which all of humanity through grace in a covenant relation with the head, Christ, are not only joined to the body of Christ, but participate

in Christ in such a way that we form a single being" ("Communion Ecclesiology: Source of Hope, Source of Controversy," *Pro Ecclesia* 2, no. 4 [1993]: 425). From this it further follows, as Walter Kaspter writes, that "the slogan: 'Jesus, yes—the Church, no'...cannot be used by either Catholic or Protestant theology. Christology and ecclesiology cannot be separated" (Joseph A. Burgess, ed., *In Search of Christian Unity: Basic Consensus/Basic Differences* [Minneapolis: Fortress, 1991], 31). "*Totus Christus* is to be sharply distinguished from that of *Christus prolongatus*, ...which Protestant theologians often unjustly accuse Catholics of holding. Whereas the first stresses the distinction between Christ as head and the Church as the body of Christ and subordinates the body to the head, the second extends Christology into ecclesiology" (p. 43).

25. J. M. R. Tillard, O.P., *Church of Churches: The Ecclesiology of Communion*, trans. R. C. DePeaux, O. Praem. (Collegeville, MN: The Liturgical Press, 1992), 70.

26. Kallistos Ware, *The Orthodox Way* (Crestwood, NY: St. Vladimir's Orthodox Theological Seminary, 1979), 107.

27. Robert W. Jenson, *Unbaptized God: The Basic Flaw in Ecumenical Theology* (Minneapolis: Fortress, 1992), 40.

28. Ibid., 97.

29. Daphne Hampson, *Christian Contradictions: The Structures of Lutheran and Catholic Thought* (Cambridge, U.K.: Cambridge University Press, 2001).

8. SIGN OR GUARANTEE?

1. This paragraph and the preceding are drawn from John Paul II's encyclical, *Ut Unum Sint* accessed on February 22, 2017, http://w2.vatican.va/content/john-paul-ii/en/encyclicals/documents/hf_jp-ii_enc_25051995_ut-unum-sint.html.

2. Robert W. Jenson, *Systematic Theology*, 2 vols. (New York and Oxford: Oxford University Press, 1997), 1:108–14.

3. *LW*, 32:24.

4. Ignatius, "To the Smyrnaeans," 6, in *The Apostolic Fathers*: Revised Greek Texts with Introductions and English Translations, ed. J. B. Lightfoot and J. R. Harner (Grand Rapids, MI: Baker Book House, 1984).

5. Italicized statements hereafter in this chapter are taken from *Declaration on the Way: Church, Ministry, and Eucharist.*

6. Kolb and Wengert, ed., *Book of Concord*, 308.

9. ON THE WAY TO CHRISTIAN PERFECTION

In reference to the World Methodist Conference signing on to the Joint Declaration, see Pontifical Council for Promoting Christian Unity, "The World Methodist Council Statement of Association with the Joint Declaration on the Doctrine of Justification," July 23, 2006, http://www.vatican.va /roman_curia/pontifical_councils/chrstuni/meth-council-docs/rc_pc_chrstuni _doc_20060723_text-association_en.html. All italicized text in this chapter is drawn from this document.

1. Martin Luther, "Preface to Romans," *The Works of Martin Luther*, vol. 6 (Philadelphia: Muhlenberg Press, 1932), 447–62; accessed January 12, 2017, http://www.messiahskingdom.com/resources/The-Gospel/luther-romans.pdf.

2. Barry E. Bryant, "Original Sin," chap. 30 in *The Oxford Handbook of Methodist Studies*, ed. William J. Abraham and James E. Kirby (Oxford, UK: Oxford University Press, 2009), 535–56.

3. John Wesley, Sermon 85, "On Working Out Our Own Salvation," in *The Bicentennial Edition of the Works of John Wesley*, ed. Albert C. Outler (Nashville: Abingdon Press, 1986), 3:199–209.

4. Martin Brecht, *Martin Luther: The Preservation of the Church, 1532–1546*, trans. J. L. Schaaf (Minneapolis: Fortress, 1993), 253–58.

5. Wesley, "On Working Out Our Own Salvation," 3:199–209.

6. Philip Jacob Spener, *Pia Desideria*, trans. Theordore G. Tappert (Philadelphia: Fortress, 1964), 49.

7. Ibid., 57–58.

8. John Wesley, "To Penelope (Madan) Maitland," in *The Bicentiennal Edition of the Works of John Wesley*, ed. Ted A. Campbell (Nashville: Abingdon Press, 2015), 27: 333. Thanks to the editor for this reference.

9. Brecht, *Preservation*, 258–62.

Afterword

1. See the breakthrough act in this regard, *Healing Memories: Reconciling in Christ* (Geneva and Strasbourg: The Lutheran World Federation and the Mennonite World Conference, 2010).

2. Gregory Sobolewski, *Martin Luther: Roman Catholic Prophet* (Milwaukee: Marquette University Press, 2001) all but comes to this conclusion.

CPSIA information can be obtained
at www.ICGtesting.com
Printed in the USA
LVOW03s1931040417

529622LV00001B/1/P